WITHDRAWN

Franziska Hillmer

Effective Sustainability Communication for Music Festivals and other Mega-Events

Find out how to Green the Crowd

Anchor Academic
Publishing

Hillmer, Franziska: Effective Sustainability Communication for Music Festivals and other Mega-Events. Find out how to Green the Crowd, Hamburg, Anchor Academic Publishing 2016

Buch-ISBN: 978-3-95489-498-7
PDF-eBook-ISBN: 978-3-95489-998-2
Druck/Herstellung: Anchor Academic Publishing, Hamburg, 2016

Bibliografische Information der Deutschen Nationalbibliothek:
Die Deutsche Nationalbibliothek verzeichnet diese Publikation in der Deutschen Nationalbibliografie; detaillierte bibliografische Daten sind im Internet über http://dnb.d-nb.de abrufbar.

Bibliographical Information of the German National Library:
The German National Library lists this publication in the German National Bibliography. Detailed bibliographic data can be found at: http://dnb.d-nb.de

---

© Anchor Academic Publishing, Imprint der Diplomica Verlag GmbH
Hermannstal 119k, 22119 Hamburg
http://www.diplomica-verlag.de, Hamburg 2016
Printed in Germany

"People come in their millions upon millions to our shows and we have the enviable position of a captive and receptive audience. We are in a position to champion causes, highlight issues and inspire changing behaviour."

(Event Professional Megan Jones 2010: vi)

List of Contents

List of Abbreviations

AGFA	A Greener Festival Award
B2B	Business to Business
BGG	Big Green Gathering Festival
BMU	Bundesministerium für Umwelt Naturschutz und Reaktorsicherheit
BTL	Below the line
CASSE	Center for the Advancement of the Steady State Economy
BCF	Big Chill Festival
CF	Coachella Festival
CFC	Chlorofluorocarbon
COP 6	Sixth Ordinary Meeting of the Conference of the Parties to the Convention on Biological Diversity
DEFRA	Department for Environment, Food and Rural Affairs (UK)
DFB	Deutscher Fußballbund
DGAP	Deutsche Gesellschaft für Ad-hoc-Publizität mbH
DVR	Deutscher Verkehrssicherheitsrat
EC	Ecocamping Assoziation
EFA	European Festival Award
FB	Facebook
FF	Falls Festival
G8	Group of Eight, forum for eight governments of major economies
GF	Glastonbury Festival
GP	Greenpeace
GfK	Gesellschaft für Konsumforschung
GMI	Green Music Initiative
GV	The Green Village Music & Arts Festival
Idkv	Bundesverband der Veranstaltungswirtschaft e.V.
IPCC	Intergovernmental Panel on Climate Change
IUCN	International Union for Conservation of Nature
JB	Julie's Bicycle
kWh	Kilowatt hour
KPI	Key Performance Indicator
LF	Latitude Festival
LiB	Lightning in a Bottle Festival
MEA	Millennium Ecosystem Assessment
MSD	MS Dockville Festival
NGO	Non-Government Organization
PET	Polyethylene terephthalate
PF	Peatsridge Festival
ppm	Parts per million

Q.	Question
RF	Rothbury Festival
RK	RheinKultur
SC	Sustainability Communication
SD	Sustainable Development
SF	Shambala Festival
SRU	Sachverständigenrat für Umweltfragen
TEEB	The Economics of Ecosystems and Biodiversity
UN	United Nations
UWF	Umweltwirtschaftsforum
VIP	Very Important Person
WCED	World Commission on Environment and Development

List of Figures

List of Tables

1. Introduction

What do you have in mind, when you hear *music festival*? Do you think on the first representatives, like Woodstock, as a movement of love and peace against the confrontational direction of the world leaders? Or, more likely, do you think of young adults hanging around without any political intentions? Festivals today are more popular than ever in Germany, but lack the revolutionary spirit of their meaningful ancestors.

But thereby mankind is confronted with the greatest challenges, which indeed are communicated by politicians and business leaders, but not satisfactorily tackled. Weather extremes all over the world remind us, with increasing frequency, of the strong dependence of human activities on climate conditions. Climate change has already begun and it looks like it will affect the living generation. These are self-made problems, because they concern those who emit more and more carbon dioxide and use so much of the natural resources that the available amount shrinks drama-tically (see Sachs 2008: 19 et seq.).

With the rising public awareness for sustainability the companies' interest to include the topic in their communications strategy has increased, which is also true for the music event industry. But while many companies are concentrated rather on green washing than acting like that, some encouraged sustainability efforts do not become public after all, although marketing communication provides a valuable tool for the strategic positioning and is able to inspire people to modify their consumption behaviour (see Meiländer 2011: 52).

Hence, this research study attempts to explore, by taking the example of Open Air Music Festivals, how an applied target group specific Sustainability Communication (SC) concept needs to be designed to reach the customer and influence them towards a more sustainable behaviour.

For research the event industry has been chosen, as it is indeed a small part of the market, but with creative and experimental characters, who could probably push greener alternatives into the limelight (see Jones 2010: 140). As there are various differences between the existing events, Open Air Music Festivals are focused as all of them have similar characteristics and attract many people, especially the younger generation, which should be aware of the sustainability challenges.

Taking results for sustainability management and the festival fans attitude into account, operators can achieve cost reductions and image improvements. As representatives of an extravagant industry they could show responsibility and tie in with the spirit of the first festivals. Ideally, it would induce more competitors to adapt to a more sustainable way.

To provide a solid foundation, the second chapter explains sustainability and how it is understood in this study, giving an overview about the present challenges regarding sustainability and named reasons. After that it takes a look at the discussed sustainability strategies to understand the field of duties the businesses face. Chapter three covers the background information about Sustainability Communication, including the role of Communication in Marketing, the specialties and action fields of SC and the respective importance of reliability. Afterwards, the fourth chapter deals with insights of the Music Event branch and the development, as well as the meaning of Open Air Music Festivals to understand their societal and economic importance and the potential to influence individuals through those events. Chapter five demonstrates the festivals' deep impact on sustainability issues, but also the few and even growing rays of hope, in the festival landscape.

The following chapter six is dedicated to combine the three different parts SC and Open Air Music Festivals. In this landscape SC strategies are analysed, to see how they are being successfully put into practice with respective to convince festival attendees.

Chapter seven describes the results from the festival fans survey examining their attitude and how this influences the SC design, especially how to encourage them, without constraining the attractiveness of the event. Therefore, promising festival communication measures become integrated. As music festival fans are from every segment of society, the results offer information about the general ecological awareness of the mostly younger generations. Due to the results a communication concept is presented at the end giving an overview about adequate measures.

The final chapter summarizes the general results of the thesis, evaluating the overall outcome of the research.

2. Sustainability Issues

As there are quite different understandings of sustainability, this initial chapter begins by defining the term and goes on to give an overview of the challenges in the sustainability discussion. It examines sustainability deficits, which arise as consequences of our economic system and the different strategies for a sustainable development (SD). This overview is helpful in understanding the complexity of the sustainability discussion and how many different aspects need to be considered when both implementing and communicating a sustainability strategy.

2.1.   Understanding Sustainability

Some people might think sustainability is a buzz word meaning nearly everything picked up by businesses to show their good will. But the first approach for sustainable development (SD) was already described in 1713 by the German Carl von Carlowitz, who in his book *Sylvicultura oeconomica* coined the forestry based definition of the term. In his understanding the conservation of natural resources is the elementary issue of sustainability, which simply means that enough resources have to remain unaffected to enable the necessary reproduction processes (see Carlowitz 1713: 105 et seq.). This descended into obscurity as industrialization progressed and technical innovations in western nations enabled humans to vastly improve living conditions. The importance of the term sustainability arose again in the sixties with observable global environmental problems and the rise of the environmental movement. Meadows et al recognized during this time that natural systems, which underpin society, will collapse soon, if resource intensive industrial development continues (see Meadows et al 1972). At this time a SD was understood as an eco-centric approach to preserve ecosystem (IUCN 1980: 18 et seq.).

The transformation to an anthropocentric view arose finally with the reuse in the *Brundtland Report* in 1987 due to the cognition of anthropogenic environmental changes caused by human mismatched manners to the requirement of livelihood (see Kruse 2005: 111). This report established a definition for SD, which is the most used: "*Sustainable development is a development that meets the needs of the present without compromising the ability of future generations to meet their own needs*", (Hauff 1987: 46). Its main aspects are resource extraction, demographic growth and assimilation ability of ecological systems, wherefore it provides recommendations for action. Furthermore, aspects are divided into consideration of intergenerational justice and distribution between developed and developing countries based on Rawls' theory of justice (see Rawls 1971).

But since then significant changes have still not been achieved. Measures to tackle climate change relocate the problems in the south hemisphere rather than solving them. The economic upturn of development countries goes in line with massive environmental destructions and a still increasing energy demand. Established in western countries are a schizophrenic attitude, political and economic proclamation of climate protection, but also the expansion of airports (and their low cost airlines), conventional power stations and international instead of national business (see Sachs 2006: 19 et seq.).

During the underlying attempt to combine SD with economic growth, the conception is also called triple bottom line approach (see figure 1), expressing that the three inter-dependent constraints must be balanced to achieve sustainability. Based on this a huge step was taken by the UN *Conference on Environment and Development* in Rio de Janeiro 1992. There, the international community determined a collection of instruments of great SD importance to step into the international political and business activities (UNEP 1992). Revolutionarily, for the first time humans were placed in focus as the affected, as well as the responsible actors (see Severin 2005: 66). Hence, national environmental policy developed into a global issue connecting environmental and development policy; which faces the important role of industrialized countries to develop sustainable lifestyles. So, the introduced UN action program, *Agenda 21*, includes a part, where all societal groups are invoked to support the conversion of the world economy. This means developing forms of consumption and production, which are bearable for the natural livelihood base (see Wehrspaun/Wehrspaun 2005: 55).

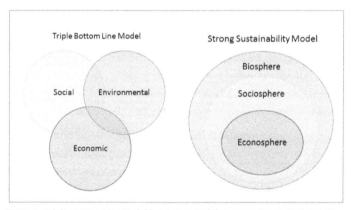

Figure 1: Triple, Bottom Line Model/Weak Sustainability versus Strong Sustainability, Source: Author, following Phase 2, The Strong Sustainability Think Tank.

By introducing the triple bottom line approach in Rio, the German Advisory Council on the Environment acknowledged the large contribution to enhance the environmental issues (see SRU 2002: 67 et seq.). Nevertheless, this idea leads to a problem:

"While a broad framing of the sustainability concept allows for a diversified and wide-ranging participation of stakeholder in the implementation of sustainability, this vagueness also leaves it open to being misused by power groups who want to press their business-as-usual attitude into a new trendy setting", (Ott et al 2011: 14).

As actors have not adequately taken into account the long term preservation of the natural capital, the triple bottom line approach has been recognized as the weak model for sustainability. It is characterized by economists strong believe in the substitutability of natural capital until a minimum (see Perman 2003: 91). Meanwhile many economics follow the approach of strong sustainability, expressed through the model below on the right (see figure 1, right picture). It suggests that the economic system is dependent on the society and both are subdivisions of the environment (see Perman 2003: 92).

Based on strong sustainability, SD is an ethically motivated and normative concept demanding lifestyles, which do not endanger humans' future (see Godemann/Michelsen 2011: 5). This includes a quantitative aspect, what means to use only the quantity of resources which is reproducible, and a qualitative aspect, which means to take care of the quality of the natural capital like water, air or soil (see von Winterfeld 2007: 46). In fact, this is comprehensible, but environmental borders are hard to face in a globalized world. In the present paper sustainability is described by the strong approach, as it is essential to preserve prosperity and the Earth as an inhabitable place for the current and future generations.

2.2.   Sustainability Challenges

Sustainability challenges are various. However, due to the *Agenda 21*, the UN plan for global transformation, the main challenges are to sustain consumption and production patterns in order to stop the deterioration of the environment. This demands an adjustment of goods and services to minimize the use of natural resources, toxic materials, waste and emissions over the whole life cycle (see Agenda 21 1992: 4.3).

Beside its role as an important production resource factor, natural capital has further important functions, like life-support services or amenity services, which can hardly be substituted through human capital. The *Millennium Ecosystem Assessment Report* (2005) by Kofi Annan, past UN General Secretary, concluded that insecurity about the various environmental interconnections and its multi-functionality is problematic. It has already been observable that the disregard of regeneration processes could lead to irreversible damages comprising the loss of ecosystem services (see MEA 2005: 155 et seq.). The utility of insects demonstrates easily the financial impact of biodiversity loss. They fertilize 80 per cent of field crops and 50 per cent of flowering plants, but millions of years of convolution have adjusted nearly every plant to specific insects making substitution difficult (Buchmann/Nabhan 1996: 292). It is easy to imagine that the work done by butterflies, bucks and honeybees can nearly neither be substituted by humans nor paid.

The results of the *TEEB* program that has been launched by the G8 in 2007 to analyse the global economics benefits of biodiversity and the costs for policy inaction, shows that the world loses natural capital worth between euro 1.35 and euro 3.10 trillion every year (Griffith 2010: 17).

This is also apparent in the unmatched biodiversity goals, which were set by the Conference of the Parties to the UN *Convention of Biological Diversity* in 2002 in order to reduce the rate of biodiversity loss significantly until 2010 (see COP 6: Decision VI/26). But instead of a reduced biodiversity loss the global resource extraction increased from 1980 to 2005 with an aggregated growth rate of 45 per cent to 58 billion tons (Luther/Giljum 2010: 1). Since a few years the *Earth Overshoot Day* demonstrates the date were the sum of resource exploitation for the current year surpass the planet's ability for reproduction, which was in 2015 already on the 13th of August. Afterwards, the deficit is made up by using the natural saving stock, adding waste and emissions in the atmosphere and the oceans (see Freeling 2011). Hence, it needs to be faced that natural systems are extremely fragile, but urgently needed to ensure human life on earth.

Actually, the demand for limited resources like coal and steel is still growing, putting even more pressure on the ecosystems and global economies (see Supersberger/Luhmann 2008: 45 et seq.).

According to *IPCC report*, the main causes of changes in temperature and rainfalls are emissions of fossil fuel burning and the massive deforestation of tropical rainforest. Globally allocated old forests, fenlands, water masses and sediments of the deep sea are as well very important permanent reservoirs for carbon dioxide (see IPCC 2007a: ch. 7). Some regions of the earth, like the Tropical Andes, shelter a rich and diverse biodiversity[1], but coeval they show a very sensitive reaction in case of changes in natural conditions (see IPCC 2007b: ch. 1.3.1). Meinshausen emphasises that the pre-industrial CO_2–equivalent-concentration of 278 parts per million (ppm) has increased to 380 ppm in 2008 and a further annual rise of two ppm is expected. Owing to this number, the concentration will very likely rise over a CO_2- equivalent of 400 ppm, the calculated upper limit to get climate change under control. Some scientists believe, it could be endurable for a short time and it would be rather important to keep the rise below an average temperature of two degrees Celsius. However, if emissions cannot be dropped, it is very likely that world climate will become uncontrollable (see Meinshausen 2008: 20 et seq.).

However, damaging nature and bringing climate into crisis are results of our present attitude. The following pages illuminate the economic reasons for the significant human influence in natural conditions.

2.3.   Economic Roots of the Struggles

It is likely that the majority of people dislike the destruction of nature. An interesting view on this allows a survey by *forsa* about preferred living conditions. The main response was 'closeness to nature', which shows the importance of Biodiversity just for a feeling of well-being (BMU 2007). This becomes even more obvious with a look at the top three issues on Germans' political agenda (see figure 2).

---

[1] See for more details http://www.biodiversityhotspots.org.

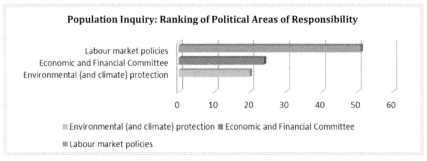

Population Inquiry: Ranking of Political Areas of Responsibility

Figure 2: Population Inquiry: Ranking of Political Areas of Responsibility; Source: Author, following BMU (2010: 16).

Intrinsically, it is not quite astonishing. A least, humans are used to life directly in and around nature. Reasons for breaking the course are mainly due to great technological achievements.

Technological progresses has led to a strengthening of the private economy, always accompanied by economists, which analyses the theoretical structures of businesses. The deep societal support for private businesses has been established since wealthy business men helped to disempower the seigniors. This was crucial to enable democracy (Böhm 1966: 75 et seq.). Once Adam Smith reduces the role of the state to an invisible hand and argues that additional value of one entrepreneur supports the overall prosperity (see Smith 1776), the belief in a successful market mechanism as the mainstreaming economic view was set. Later, Malthus (1798) remarked that the availability of land or natural resources as a reason for population growth, but also as the limiting factor for a further expansion. The decline of marginal earnings would lead to a further decrease of population until a steady state. Ricardo (1817) faced this problem as well, but presented the rising of the intensive or extensive margin of land as solution for avoiding resource scarcity. This led to his famous perception of the comparative advantage against the background of the introduction of protective duties in Great Britain. It means that companies should focus on those goods, which can be produced more cost-effectively than others. In addition to these ideas, the inclusion of fossil fuels pushed the rapid growth of technological progress and knowledge, so that an on-going technological improvement and specialization were seen, until today, as the favoured solution for capacity problems or bottlenecks (Perman et al 2003: 5). Very soon there was not only the challenge to deliver enough resources for a still growing population, but also to keep the accrued industry, which entails jobs and high investments.

There was also a change in economic theory. The representatives of the *classical national economy*, like the mentioned men, have seen the production value in the output as a result of labour. The *neoclassical* view puts more emphasis on the trading process, where values are relative and were set by supply and demand (Perman et al 2003: 3). Further inspired by Vilfredo Paretos' studies on economic efficiency, businesses have been in a permanent state of trying to reach a higher efficiency. Even if some challenges arose in terms of economic crisis, never the path itself was

19

questioned; rather the way in which to strengthen it. Hence, John Maynard Keynes reintroduced the important role of the state, in order to set adequate incentives for stimulating economic growth (1936).

A look at the neoclassical theories presents more analysis, which have shown that specialization, so in the *Neoclassical Trade Theory by inter-sectorial trade* (Ohlin 1923) or in the *New Trade Theory* by *intra-sectorial trade* (Krugman 2009) could encourage growth and higher welfare effects. So, it leads to outsourcing, centralization and finally to supply chains extended over the globe. But beside the fact that it becomes risky to align on long distance supply chains, which conceivably will be restricted by rising oil prices or institutional limitation of allowed emissions, multinational companies, some of them stronger than states, continue to accelerate resource exploitation. DeSombre considers that avoiding environmental pollution is costly for the firms. Hence, should pollution damages for the local society arise, it normally does not affect the businesses directly. So they can remove valuable natural resources and move on after they have exploited a region. The business managers in their position feel unable to care for it as they are responsible for the successful performance of their businesses, demanding a large amount of capital and therefore investors, who need to be convinced. Typically, high profits are the best argument for them, explaining the on-going need for growth and creating new products to create new customer demands. There it comes to the economic creative destruction as Schumpeter named the entrepreneurial process (see Schumpeter 1942: 136 et seq.), but occurring much more intensively in another way, which is graphically summarized by Professor Bardi (see figure 3):

However, there is no doubt that, despite the societal fallouts, the industrialized countries were able to achieved high welfare effects in the second half of the 20th century, which goes in line with social balance measures. Some may wave criticism aside and say nothing is perfect, but it has come to further maldevelopments.

To make profitable earnings it was beneficial that the financial sector has introduced low interest rates in the last decades and has steadily reduced controlling tools for the financial risks management. Hence, seeing the opportunity for investment combined with the unflappable belief in personal luck and nearly uncontrolled markets led to the burst of market bubbles (see Ricciardi 2008).

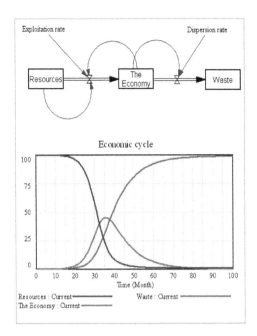

Figure 3: Simply Economic Model Based on System Dynamics (upper picture) and the Change of Stock Size in Time; Source: Bardi (2011).

As a result many people are scared to lose their capital assets and the national states still try to handle the latest economic crisis. The continuous globalisation process with the associated cost pressure is challenging for many enterprises in the industrialized countries, because their home based production centres are not able to produce as cheaply as foreign located ones with lower social welfare systems and less environmental regulations. This is especially puzzling for regional enterprises. Usually those have a smaller carbon foot print - an advantage in sustainable terms - and support domestic social structures. But they cannot afford the low prices, which have become possible through mass production and global outsourcing.

Hence, it results in higher unemployment rates and a tremendous change of established social structures. Employees get used to moving to another big city or even other countries every couple of years, where multinational companies promise well-paid jobs. They also get used to commuting, accept low wages, long working hours and are often still frightened to lose their jobs, as many are just temporary. This development leads to negative impacts on families, regions (de- and overpopulation), climate and even democratic structures (see Schemel 2010). Where multinational companies offer jobs and dominate markets, it is clear that political institutions are hesitating to set rules, which might disperse powerful actors. That is why some experts see that these evolutions lead to a *"loss of policy autonomy"* (Milner/Keohane 1996: 16 et seq.). Schemel argues that productivity has been grown so much that firms need to expand to keep the same amount of jobs.

Since then the tasks of the institutions switched from regulation and control to deregulation and liberation of the market forces, which would endanger the civil rights and liberties what people fought for in the last centuries (cf. Schemel, 2010: 84 et seq.). The line of arguments from other globalization critics like Stiglitz (i.e. 2003) or Ziegler (2003) goes in a similar direction.

It becomes clear that the reviewed crisis are strongly linked to each other and that they need a comprehensive approach for a solution.

2.4.   Strategies for a Sustainable Development

For decades many economics have asked, whether this direction is still welfare supporting. So, Keneth Boulding, broadly seen as one of the founding fathers of *Ecological Economics* (see Perman et al 2003: 9), remembered with his publication *The Economics of the Coming Spaceship Earth* that the economy is a subsystem of a larger system. He suggested other models instead of the neoclassical growth paradigm, wherein less production and consumption are key issues (see 1966: 3 et seq.). John Maynard Keynes was convinced that growth is necessary, but only until economic problems become solved (see 1930). Thus, Ecological Economists have worked on bringing sustainable problems into economics and have developed different approaches to find economic solutions for these challenges, particularly as the sustainable problems have to intervene the international business activities the one or the other way around (see Sarkis 2010: 78 et seq.).

The sustainable theory distinguishes between three different ways to realize sustainability. These three indicatory concepts are *efficiency, consistency* and *sufficiency* (see Huber 1995).

Efficiency means to achieve an economic goal, like producing a good, with the least possible resource and energy input; for instance as proclaimed by the *Faktor 4* approach (see Weizsäcker/Lovins/Lovins 1995). Hence, revenue and effort become optimized and enable businesses to reduce resource costs. Typical measures are adapting efficient technologies or resource recycling. But, efficiency needs to be valued adequately. Otherwise utility, which is of course bound to specific interests and prospects, cannot be determined (see Scholz 1996: 4). So even cars in Germany, which emit much more than others, get a green sticker (meaning the most harmless emission group) due to the specific categorization.

This examples with respect to a still rising world population makes decoupling, the basic idea of the green new deal, just a wishful thinking, unless *"growth in the richer nations is curtailed, or some kind of completely unforeseen technological breakthrough happens"*, (Jackson 2011: 86). The argumentation of Hawken et al (1999) goes in the same direction, when they say:

> *"Without a fundamental rethinking of the structure and the reward system of commerce, narrowly focused eco-efficiency could be a disaster for the environment by overwhelming resource savings with even larger growth in the production of the wrong products (...), using the wrong business models",*
>
> (Hawken et al 1999: x)

However, the efficiency strategy is in line with the political and economic growth attempts and with the UN definition of sustainable development.

Realizing efficiency problems, the approach of ecological *consistency*, sometimes also called *eco-effectiveness* was set (see Braungart/Mc Donough 2002: 72). Their underlying concept of *cradle-to-cradle* is the idea of removing waste through the reuse of residues for another process. This technological and innovative oriented approach is focused on natural metabolic cycles, describing a qualitative change to nature-identical products and technologies (see Huber 1995: 111 et seq.). Hence, it is not an attempt to produce less, jut differently. Especially, the idea of biomimicry in the field of green chemistry engineering raises hope (see Doble/Kruthiventi 2007).

Due to rising population growth, Grunwald sees this strategy as essential, especially regarding the energy demands, and sees the use of hydrogen instead of fossil fuels as a supreme example for *consistency*, because there are no negative effects probable, even with an extensive usage (2003: 223 et seq.). Further, he rejects concepts, which postulate Bio-fuels or so called clean coal as too lavish and backward oriented (see Grunwald 2003: 225). However, Paech argues that the consistency strategies would be used as the best alibi to go on with a continuous economic growth (see 2005: 55). This could be harmful, while improvements cannot automatically reduce the consumption, they could moreover trigger the rise in resource use to a higher request, so called backfire-effect (see Herring/Sorrell 2009). Nevertheless, *consistency* is able to achieve a relative decoupling between a rise in consumption and the growth of environmental pressure due to the decline of environmental inputs per unit, but leads not mandatory to an absolute decoupling (see Grosse 2010).

The third orientation is the one with the most negative denotation as many people associate it with the switch from well-loved behaviours towards an ascetic life-style: *Sufficiency*, (Winterfeld 2007: 48). Asserted by Daly (1996) also Scherhorn promotes a modest life-style including a general reduction of resource expenditure as well as the regionalization and deceleration of production, consumption and traffic as well as the partial removal of industry. Emphasized is the individual redevelopment of agricultural and mechanical skills (see 1997: 25 et seq.). Fitting to this, a redevelopment of regional economic cycles is a recommended resilience strategy to handle globali-sation crisis like peak oil, climate change, financial crisis and accordingly to enforce the local economic and social structures (see Paech 2005: 67).

Princen explains the concept of sufficiency from another perspective: When individuals doing something, for instance eating, sleeping, or consumption, they reach a saturation point. Then, surplus value changes into negative effects. So, sufficiency would mean to consume an adequate amount for an optimal well-being, which means in fact downsizing consumption and the typical high living standard (see Princen 2003: 43). Therefore, energy and resource use can be rapidly diminished, already by changing extravagant private life styles. Rogall demonstrates this with examples like jogging instead of skiing, buying second hand products or avoidance of car use (see 2004: 127 et seq.). But Grunwald argues sufficiency had only a low acceptance, which would invalidate the topic pragmatically (see Grunwald 2003: 219). Alcott claims shifting effects, for instance the decrease of meat consumption in one region could lead to a rising demand in other regions, where it thereto becomes affordable to buy meat (see 2008: 770 et seq.). Korhonen remarks in addition that sufficiency needs a regional diversity of suppliers and demanders, products and services (see 2005: 35 et seq.). The less compatibility of economic extension and sufficiency is also mentioned by Winterfeld. She sees the problem that new streets and shopping centre were built to increase consumption, but otherwise people should be advised to use it only moderately to enable sustainable development (see 2007: 54).

Indeed, sufficiency demands a radical change in used behaviour. Paech explains that sufficiency demands the questioning of own wants, validating what is really necessary to meet own needs and casting off any unnecessary burdened ballast, which is taking time, money, nerves and ecological resources. Therefore, a cultural change is needed, where the society is no longer dominated by rising material welfare, which is already overloading the daily life. Hence, if more things are self-made, people re-obtain self-determination, as they reduce insecurities due to less dependence on monetary inputs (see Paech 2010: 232 et seq.).

Lucas and Matys describe culture as a diverse societal value system, which evolves through societal praxis. They suggest a change in the value system, but see conflicts by the short-winded political management system (see 2003: 12 et seq.). To achieve cultural change, the market surrounding institutional context is targeted in particular to implement a sustainable de-commoditization strategy. It emphasizes the influences of goods and limiting the commercialization effect (see Hirsch 1967: 84).

However, the present level of consumption is stimulated by the socio-cultural conception of well-being and happiness that supports the materialistic more than non-materialist values (see Brown/Cameron 2000: 34). An idea to reach sustainable development was made by Daly (1996) with his *steady state economy*. It demands resources extraction that stays within the regeneration and assimilation limits. He was a student of Georgescu-Roegen, who is broadly seen as the inventor of a *degrowth* vision by referring to the *Second Law of Thermodynamic* (1971). Jackson talks about *Prosperity without Growth* (2010) and advises the strengthening of social capital. It includes mainly (de-)regionalization processes, reducing geographical labour mobility and claims more responsibilities to local communities (see Jackson 2010: 183). Furthermore, he mentions that the consumerism culture needs to be degraded to stop people *"seek[ing] identity and search[ing] for meaning through material goods"*, (2012: 183).

Paech, as a proponent of *post-growth* economics, sees concepts such as Community Supported Agri-culture[2], regional decentralized energy supply or regional currencies reinforce the regions economically and in an environmental friendly way so that people are able to reduce the dependence on national or international businesses. Long product life cycles and an increase in use intensity should finally lead to a material zero-sum game (Paech 2009: 26 et seq.). Paech points out that "*Markets, entrepreneurs, money, consumer goods and technological innovations would still be necessary in a post-growth economy – but far from a culture of exorbitance*", (Paech 2009: 27).

In fact, sustainable development, as it is seen by the UN, and degrowth are opposites. Interestingly, the representatives of a steady state economy say that according to the individual economics distance to the natural limit an "*economy can reach a steady state after a period of growth or after a period of downsizing or degrowth*", (CASSE 2011). It is crucial to understand that degrowth does not mean to go back to the Stone Age, but rather to re-obtain life in accord with natural laws, which is just the assumption Malthus made 200 years ago (see p. 7). Nevertheless, it is problematic to sell the new approach to the neoclassical economists, where degrowth means nothing else than recession combined with unemployment and massive financial injections.

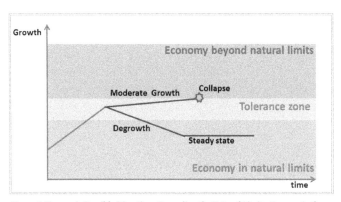

Figure 4: Economic Possible Directions Regarding the Natural Limits; Source: Author.

Nevertheless, if 20 per cent of the humans on earth consume 80 per cent of the worlds' resources than it is not possible that 50 or 100 per cent live in the same way, not even with a focus on ecological modernization. So, Alcott says, a mixed strategy is needed to achieve a sustainable way of consumption, consisting of the presented components efficiency, consistency and sufficiency, induced by a change of the culture, which includes a decrease in the level of consumption. He summarizes it by saying that consumers from rich western countries need to consume less (sufficiency) but more efficient and also differently (de-commoditization) (see Alcott 2008: 786).

---

[2] Meanwhile fast growing recovery, observable for instance at this online farm directory for the United States: http://www.localharvest.org/.

Therefore, sustainability communication plays an important role in different parts of society in order to manifest the change. What this means is revisited in the following chapter.

3. Basis of Sustainability Communication

Looking at the previous chapter, one of the most important issues is it to find ways for spreading the needs for a SD society wide. Therefore, the current chapter first looks at the role of communication in business marketing and investigates the meaning of sustainability communication afterwards. Before strategies and instruments were presented, the general bottlenecks within sustainability communication become examined to analyse the challenges for businesses in the final part.

3.1.   Communication and Marketing

In general, communication was termed by Ziemann as the principle of societal organization itself, due to its important role in spreading information among social creatures (Ziemann 2007: 124). Watzlawick decisively influenced the communication research by its *axiom of human communication*. The first and most famous axiom *one cannot not communicate*, demonstrates the broad influence of communication. It simply means nobody can avoid communication, no matter whether something has been said or not. Every activity sends a message (see Watzlawick 1967: 48 et seq.).

Within business communication policy is, beside market research, product policy, distribution policy and contracting policy, an important marketing instrument geared to anticipate, awake and meet the needs of the customers (see Weis 2007: 14). It contains the planned creation and transmission of information directed towards the market to influence opinions, attitude and behaviour in favour of companies (see Diller 2001: 791). Pepels adds that it means to adjust the opinion reality of the own purposive idea (see 2005: 25). Companies inform customers, potential customers and the interested society about products or services as well as about the company. Thereby they try to meet their needs (see Thommen/Achleitner 2006: 258).

Jossè et al state moreover that structurally, marketing communication is a part of push communication, meaning a unilateral communication from sender to receiver that should raise publicity, exposing the unique selling point and increasing the willingness to buy or increase sympathy for the brand or the company respectively (see 2011: 6). Nevertheless, it could absolutely generate a pull effect at the receivers' site. Thus, the receiver wants to buy or at least to get more information about the product or service. Thereby it should be artful designed to raise attention. Furthermore they indicate the importance of planning and controlling in marketing communication (see Jossè et al 2011: 3).

Hence, the communication process here is an exchange between individuals or groups of individuals, but with the senders' conscious intension to influence the recipients. Traditionally marketing communication includes five core instruments: Advertisement, Public Relations, Sales Promotion, Personal Selling and Direct Marketing (see Meffert/Kirchgeorg 1998: 316 et seq.).

Weis complements modern Instruments: Sponsoring, Product Placement and Online Advertising (see Weis 2007: 181). Rheinländer et al refer to the growing importance of *social media* for communications and the chances for sustainability communication (see 2011: 95 et seq.).

3.2. Meaning

Godemann and Michelsen assert that humans should take responsibility and restructure their relationships to each other and to nature (see 2011: 4) and explain what it needs:

> "*This requires a social process of mutual understanding that deals with both the causes of these development and their possible solutions. In other words, a process of communication and mutual understanding that is also known as sustainability communication,* (Godemann/Michelsen 2011: 4).

They further emphasise that sustainability communication (SC) deals "*with the future development of society at the core of which is a vision of sustainability.*" (2011: 6). From the theoretical perspective SC is obviously influenced by Communication theory, but as well by various other scientific disciplines like Systems theory, Epistemology Constructivism, Media Theory, Cultural Theory of Risk and Sociology. Until now no own theory exists for SC (see Godemann/Michelsen 2011: 7- 11)

Since the Rio Summit established the principle of sustainable development (see p. 3), nature conservation is not longer the key medium for ecological communication, but rather sustainable development (Siebert 2005: 133). Also taken into account are norms like inter- and intra-generational justice, cause study or perception of challenges. Further the action taking and influencing possibilities on a societal and individual base are taking place in various parts of the society. The basis of this communication is that concrete challenges evoking a non-sustainable development on a regional, national and international level (see Michelsen 2005: 27 et seq.). Regarding its appearance say Godemann and Michelsen, SC "*is found in fields of discourse that includes all social systems [...], such as politics, law, science, business or education*" (2011: 10).

But until now the distribution of the notion sustainable development is not successful. Even if political discussion has dealt with it since 1987, knew in 1998 only 15 per cent and in 2004 with a slight increase 22 per cent of the German population this notion, depending very much on the educational level. It demonstrates that the general public has still not been adequately informed that it is not just about environmentalism, but about implementing cultural change and sustainable consumption patterns (see Wehrspaun/Wehrspaun 2005: 56). Indeed, the confusing utilization and the different approaches in the scientific fields do not make it easier to understand the meaning. Nevertheless, it occurs a large identification with its principles like resource conservation, fair trade or inter-generational justice (see 2005: 203). The BMU examined as well that people do have a strong connection to nature and that environmentalism is relevant for them, as well if they do not behave like that, because mostly they cannot grasp or ignore their own responsibility (see BMU 2010: 35).

3.3.   Bottlenecks

Due to this resonance in society, it can be faced that environmentalism alone is not enough to foster a sustainable development (see Kruse 2005: 110 et seq.), but great potentials to further implement the needs of a strong sustainability do exist. The associated requirements concerning learning processes and the development of shaping skills are quite tough due to interactions summarized by Kruse (see 2005: 112):

- Missing human sensory organs to realize environmental changes like ozone holes or radioactive fallouts and complexity, dynamic and non-transparency of human-environment- interference are not accomplishable challenges for humans' cognitive skills;

- Impacts of environmental interferences are often delayed, delayed relatable and at long-distance; especially true for global environmental changes like emissions (CFC; CO^2) or outsourced environmental problems due to globalization;

- Own impact is deemed too low to make a difference, as the big picture is not faceable (for instance referring to car or energy usage).

Beside the fact that individuals do not feel affected, explained by the bullets points above, it further depends on personal values (individual factors), temporal emotions as well as social norms and values of a group or the society as a whole (interpersonal and social factors). Furthermore, there need to be alternative options for a sustainable action (see Kruse 2005: 115). If changing the own behaviour is too difficult, even a motivated person would not remodelling patterns.

Due to the complexity of sustainability - the notion is very abstract and does not evoke emotions in contrast to nature conservation or animal protection - it makes it difficult to use for communication processes (see Siebert 2005: 136 et seq.). To embed sustainability in the value system of a society Lucas and Matys suggest a purposeful emotional staging of the topic. Therefore it would be essential to find the right ways of presenting the topic to the society, including how to find out how sustainable moral concepts could be strengthened and how they should be communicated and staged to connect responsible businesses and individuals with a sustainable life style (Lucas/Matys, 2003: 5 et seq.).

And even if more and more people grasp particular problems, like too much energy use or meat consumption, and despite rising attention of the principles in the media, extensive information in brochures and literature, there still exists the mentioned difference between knowledge and activities (see Matthies et al 2004). Thereto, an important point to mention is that sustainable development treats frightening issues in its core and communication about risks affects the personal well-being as well as the necessity to react. Hence, people avoid to going into details or rather ignore the topics completely (see Japp 2000: 74 et seq.). That is why the media, especially the mass media, has a particular significance for a transmission of information about sustainable challenges as a tool for making complex matters concrete and understandable. It means as well that media is massively involved in shaping the societal understanding of those issues (see Kruse 2005: 13). Witt even says: "*Media do not portray reality [...], but rather generate it*", (Witt, 2005: 174).

Thus, a smart communication is essential to develop a societal sustainable development demanding the following tasks for SC, named by Wehrspaun and Wehrspaun (2005: 61 et seq.):

- Advancement of integrative thinking to develop a culture of sustainability;
- Transfer of knowledge for sustainable lifestyles should transmit practical opportunities for sustainable behaviour in the broad society by forming conciliation structures within schools, companies and local groups;
- Make tangible that the idea of sustainability needs wise habits in terms of Kant to activate the whole civil potential.

3.4.   Strategies and Instruments

To reach these goals different strategies and instruments for SD were created, mostly based on environmental psychology, which settle the way of sustainability communication. Cognition oriented strategies built on the available perception, knowledge and work with information and education, which asked for a fitting information design, communication media and personal skills of communicators.

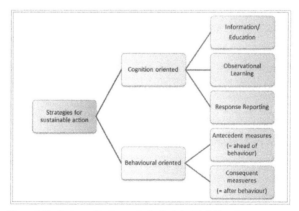

Figure 5: Strategies and Instruments for Sustainable Action; Source: Author, based on Kruse 2005: 116.

It comprises as well the response about success or failure of an action. Learning by modelling can be part of cognition-oriented strategies, but is as well an instrument of antecedent measures. Further instruments in this category are behavioural clues like signs, self- defined goals or self-obligations. Consequent measures include, for instance, incentives, punishment as well as individual or collective feedback. It is applicable to all, that instruments should be adapted to the specific target group, action fields and the circumstances to become successful (see Kruse 2005: 16 et seq.).

The organigram in figure 5 helps to face the different ways SC can emerge. Godemann and Michelsen underline the importance of Social Marketing for SC, particularly in online communication and social networks. They further mention that the marketing tools, normally used for goods or services, can be adapted more efficient and fitting to the target group. The authors also recommend the empowerment of individuals by communicative planning and participation instruments like future workshops, round tables or eParticipation. Therewith users become able to recognize non-sustainable activities and how to substitute it with sustainable alternatives. Hence, civil society could be strengthened and individuals get involved in shaping a sustainable future.

The education of SD is strongly linked to this. The difference is that learners are not just trained in changing behaviour, they should rather participate autonomously (see Godemann/Michelsen 2011: 9 et seq.). However, educational measures bear the risk of boomerang effects, when individuals do not like to get lectured (see Reisch et al 2008: 10).

Structural policy can be divided into strong instruments, like regulatory or economic measures, and soft ones, comprising of information and consulting instruments. Linked to the applicability of the demonstrated strategies, Michelsen reflects SC as part of soft structural political instruments, which he also called persuasive instruments, as they do not present obligations, but should convince people to change. He adds examples like governmental or non-governmental sustainability reporting, labelling, already mentioned initiatives and campaigns or considering of sustainability aspects in consumer tests (see Michelsen 2005: 30-32).

However, it is notably in the scientific discussion that the instruments are mainly allocated to profit or non-profit oriented actors. Hence, apart from *profit marketing* the specific marketing concept *social marketing* has been established entailing activities created for the benefit of society (Weis 2007: 21). Examples therefore are initiatives like the '*Slow Down*' campaign by the German Traffic Safety Council o.V. (DVR), financed by the Federal Ministry of Transport (see Degener 2009: 38), but as well issues of sustainability as an important concern of the society.

3.5.   Businesses Challenge

Implementing SC in businesses, Clausen and Fichter say, comprises all communication policy measures which are connected to the social and ecological impact of the business activities, and which are as well intended to communicate them among the stake holders (see 1996: 6 et seq.).

Mast and Fiedler quoted that companies pursue mainly three different ways of SC (see 2005: 572):

- Reporting, focussed on non-monetary topics;
- Permanent dialogs with critical stakeholders like NGOs, to let them participate and avoid negative headlines;
- Participation in events or own events to get in contact with important stakeholders.

Michelsen specifies the mentioned permanent dialog by allocating consulting-tools as well as co-operation and negotiation instruments (see Michelsen 2007: 27 et seq.). Furthermore Severin points out that companies' SC is focused on those stakeholders, who claim a co-determination (see Severin 2005: 66 et seq.). Information and education are rather topics for internal stakeholder communication. Thus, it can take place between the company members to raise the awareness for sustainability issues, which encourages additionally the building of shared values among the colleagues. Indeed, the internal sustainability communication has an allocative and structural function as they support the adaption of determined sustainability strategies (see Hardtke/Prehn 2001: 220).

Besides that, sustainability issues already play a role in the purchase decision as SC is used to profile the company as a responsible minded one on the market. Especially in the consumer goods market exists a high potential to gain an improved selling proposition (see Fichter 2000: 264). Nevertheless, communication itself cannot sell a product or a service, as Jossè et al mention. It cannot be convincing as long as problems in the other parts of the '*Marketing Ps*' like price or product arise (Jossé et al 2011: 6).

Moreover, it is a difficult task to gain the stakeholders trust, as market endogenous difficulties occur. The companies' liability is hard to proof for the public or the consumer. Thus, due to these information asymmetries, many companies try to exploit this advantage so that green-washing occurs.

Entrepreneurs who really try to run the businesses more sustainably are dependent on cooperation partners, which often needed to be convinced, but should also prove to be trustworthy. This further elucidates the need for a careful SC, especially in times of social media, where wrong statements get unmasked ruthlessly and even single mistakes, ones published, are hard to repair (see Jossè et al 2011: 4). However, it is a disadvantage to neglect SC as more and more companies have recognized the demand for it.

Referring to the methods of SC, the typical sustainability reporting is done through print media and internet, described by Lichtl as the classical-informative version. The reports are focused to describe the problems and the planned solutions, which are most likely attractive for stakeholders strongly involved in the topic.

To reach other target groups, he suggests the usage of classical-emotional methods meaning to awake interests at first by emotions and deliver information afterwards. Emotional-associative formats can also be created by designing new methods, which include event marketing strategies and live communication (see Lichtl 2003).

However, by comparing the efforts within the public and the private sector, companies barely overtake true responsibility for a sustainable development. What many pursue is the so-called *license to operate* by calming pressure groups that care and could demolish the image of a company (see Severin 2005: 67 et seq.). Severin quotes further the procedure of companies using CSR activities just to draw off the attention from deficits in sustainability processes and to show good will. This is undoubtedly still in line with the understanding of CSR as it is seen as a voluntary acceptance of responsibility (see Severin 2005: 72). But it remarkably has little to do with the understanding of SC remarked by Godemann and Michelsen. Hence, if businesses stuck on the proclaimed self-commitment by adding some voluntary CSR measures instead of truly integrating sustainability management by transforming things like supply chains, products and guiding principles, SC gets reduced to green washing which must lead to a lack of trust among the costumers as soon as contradictions occur.

Severin mentions that business are right to connect their CSR- initiatives with its sustainability concept as it delivers manifold opportunities to transfer the companies moral values and societal self-conception to stakeholders (see 2005: 73). Antes argumentation goes in the same direction by saying that it is essential for businesses sustainability strategy to consider two essential characteristics to present the sustainability topic convincing for the customers (following Antes 1992: 490 et seq.):

1. The direct sustainability, meaning that sustainability is persuasive and fully integrated into the business strategy and operations;
2. The indirect sustainability, implying the enabling and encouraging stakeholders to act sustainably, what specifically demands a trustful sustainable behaviour and the communication about the own efforts without green-washing elements and should furthermore include awareness- raising of sustainability issues through communication tools.

Hence, companies should inform and educate their stakeholders about the demands of sustainable development and integrate this as an important part of their SC strategy. If a company does really espouse itself for sustainable ideas by integrating a comprehensive sustainability management and implementing SD related social marketing initiatives, even if this is not inconclusively supporting business and it is or at least seems altruistic, it leads to a higher reliability. Thus, it can become a very important part of the marketing communication strategy with its typical aims like customer loyalty or image improvement.

If those activities get successfully adapted it even generates a higher consciousness for sustainability measures by those stakeholder groups, who have not thought about it yet. At least in the society there is a high identification with the sustainability principles (see p. 6), so that most are likely to be willing to change behaviour if adequate solutions get presented. And even more they are nudged to think about their activities from time to time (see Thaler/Sunstein 2009). Thereby a nudge is *"any aspect of the choice architecture that alters people's behavior in a predictable way without forbidding any options"*, (see Thaler/Sunstein 2009: 6). It could include as well the enabling of individuals in self-subsistence to reactive abilities, which are able to reduce dependences on monetary income (see p. 11). Kruse moreover remarks that communication demands to consider group and sub group specific lifestyles respective to different problem areas for estimating the potential resonance for sustainable issues (see Kruse 2005: 111).

By following the approach that SC means to achieve a more sustainable behaviour, it can be added that those measures have to be part of SC, which targeting people who normally do not think about the topic and do not necessarily speak about the sustainability challenges. Only if information and education initiatives for achieving sustainable behaviour were seen as primary ingredient in businesses SC, it will incite companies to shift away from voluntary good-will CSR-initiatives towards a really commitment to sustainability, forcing competitors to follow. Reisch et al also recognize:

> *"[A]ttempts to reaching the disinterested mass of the population with a sustainable consumption message seem relatively rare or restricted to crisis (e. g. energy or water shortages). There is then a lack of research as to the potential means and their effectiveness"*, (Reisch et al 2008: 3).

Thus, if individuals could be nudged to adapt a more sustainable behaviour (e. g. reducing meat consumption) by focussing on non-sustainability issues (Vegan food makes skinny and is healthier), SD can be supported as well. Especially advisable are arguments linked to recognition, social equality, solidarity and activities with families and friends as they are crucial aspects for a high satisfaction level and people are susceptible to those issues (see Sachs 2008: 234 et seq.).

As a result of a comprehensive SC strategy, the number of stakeholders interested in the sustainability performances rises so that the image effect increases due to additional stakeholders who care.

It becomes obvious that companies have a great responsibility for sustainable development and entail an enormous chance to support it. In this context music festivals, as part of the event culture, offer an interesting and convenient research topic for sustainability communication, as they have a high potential to reduce environmental damage. There is an influencing institutional context at the festival and there is a high interaction level with the customers from various social milieus. In front of its sustainability related research, the following chapter offers an insight into the music festival scene as important part of the music event industry.

4. Music Festivals – Special Events for the Society and the Music Event Industry

Almost no one could imagine a life without music. Countless examples of radio use, CD sales and music downloads prove the strong connection, no matter which kind of music is preferred. Sometimes music fans come together at *Open Air Music Festivals*. The present chapter will identify the general meaning of events, the development of music festivals and their significance for economy and society.

4.1. Meaning of Events

"*An event is an event is an event – but what is an event?*", asked Wünsch and Thuy (2007: 13) and suggesting to integrate the medium event among the term communication, more specific in life-communication and group-communication, which is used by management and marketing as an integrative communication strategy. Typical characteristics they have examined are a defined communication- or marketing-strategy, which has a clear message, a target group as well as a definitive occasion-, budget- and coordination- team and finally it is short-lived, even if the format is repeatable (Wünsch/Thuy 2007: 14 et seq.).

The *Political Studies Institute* remarks that after the Second World War the popular celebration has been a success of the new industrial economy. Today, festivals still play an important role in our society. Within the UK alone more than 500 festivals take place plus hundreds of community based festivals and carnivals every year (see Bowdin et al 2010: 9 et seq.).

Gerhard Schulze shaped the term *event society*, remarking the searching of individuals for happiness and the requirement to experience as much as possible within a given time frame (see Schulze 1992). Important aspects concerning people are for instance the wish to experience something special, communality or self-dramatization. Following up these argumentations, Lucas and Matys observed a trend in the event industry of an increasing usage of manifold stimuli, achieved through commercial offers, to improve the event. This would lead to a broad range of promising service and product constructions like theme parks, computer games or events (Lucas/Matys 2003: 20). But due to the attempts to increase the presented specialties and recognizable efforts, known things become boring or too many things lead to a sensual overload. Schulze recommends, especially for the media industry, to re-explore contents as own identifiers and distinguishing features (Schulze 2000: 64 et seq.). This could be ideally be filled with answers on how to create a beautiful and individually worthwhile life (Schulze 1992: 37).

Also Thuy and Wünsch recognized that within the young industry the naivete of the early- years with its as much as possible-philosophy has gone and becomes substituted by '*why and how much*' (2007: 15).

However, preconditions for such an event society would be the replacement of work and profit-based and materialistic views, by playing out the needs of the present time like individual fulfilment and pleasure, which are the sovereign form of traditional prosperity (see Hebbel-Seeger/Förster 2008: 32). Indeed, this goes in line with the sufficiency strategy of sustainable development. Lucas and Matys further illustrate that the broad media distribution of event patterns would have developed events to an integral part of the everyday culture, implying the convergence of mainstream and high culture. The medialization of society provides a surface for culture, economy and as well politics, which could be adapted depending on demand (see Lucas/Matys 2003: 26).

To examine the different approaches and possibilities it is at first necessary to take a look at the chosen area of music festivals as part of the music event industry.

Wünsch and Thuy point out the broad variety of events, depending on the kind of occasion. Hence, events can be divided for instance in business events, festivals, community events, sport events, charity events etc. (2007: 15). The different types underline the importance of those happenings in the daily life. It is the chance to convene, to exchange thoughts and ideas, to get input and to earn recognition. It is very unlikely, even in times of globalization and social media, that the events will become less important in the future.

Getz realized already in 1991, that festivals and events are part of an alternative tourism contributing to SD, probably in a broader view (see Getz 1999: 5 et seq.).

4.2.   Development of Music Festivals

In the last decades, the festival business has been one of the fastest growing divisions within the general leisure industry (see Nicholson/Pearce 2001). Confronted with increasing digital distribution of music the expansions of live performances are a good substitution for the reduction in music disc sales (see Steinkrauß et al 2008: 37 et seq.).

Music festivals, understood as an occasion where music as the reason for a happening – and no religious or legitimated power- is presented in front of a paying audience, firstly arose in the 18th century. At the end of the 19th century the emancipation movement led to the construction of pretentious concert halls. By taking part in music events the audience became part of a collective with specific behavioural codes - becoming even more particular during the differentiation by the exploration of new rhythm, styles and sounds. The reason for joining such an event is and was not only the individual taste in music, but also the possibility to be part of a community and to have the feeling of belonging (see Troendle 2009: 28 et seq.).

Basically, festivals can be divided into classical festivals and the open air festivals, where mainly young people listen to Rock, Electro and Pop music combined with an established fan culture. Open air festivals are a result of the youth culture since the 1950s, which established the *Star* cult. The numbers of visitors of famous-artist-studded-festivals rose rapidly, with great challenges for the inexperienced organizers. In the middle of the sixties the first festivals opened in Germany. Since then festivals have been greatly redefined and shaped by the concert agencies *Lippert and Rau, Mama Concerts* as well as *Carsten Jahnke Concert direction.* In 2011 more than 350 festivals took place in Germany.[3] In comparison to that, Graf enumerates that in 1993 only 183 open air concerts and festivals were held (see 1995: 245). Thus, the enthusiasm for festivals rather keeps on growing, and it is time to clarify what they mean for the society.

4.3.   Significance for Economy and Society

One third of the Germans, over the age of 10 years, visit a minimum of one music event per year. Thus, first of all festival organization is a lucrative business for the music event industry. Beside the high pricing possibilities, expenses for merchandising amount more than 17 Euro just for one visit per person. In general, the sum music fans spend on sound carrier is just the half of the sum they are willing to pay for the live performances (Pfleiderer et al 2008: 95).

Beside that the economic impact for the region where a festival takes place is comparatively low, because the most of the participants camp and eat at the festival area. The other way around the local community is confronted with very short term but intensive burden regarding public services, waste, pollution and noise exposure, which lead justifiably to conflicts. Apart from conflicts in the local area, festivals have as well a negative public image. The image problem is due to the typical public realized features of a music festival like euphoric, but also drunken, drugged and even aggressive teenagers (Pfleiderer 2008: 89 et al).

About 50 per cent of the younger generation like to visit a music festival (10-29 years; see GfK 2007: 8). It is also observable that there is still a relatively high interest to participate in music events in every age. The shift from a stronger interest to the Rock and Pop-Concerts instead of a festival visit in the age of 20 to 29 is likely due to the higher income, other priorities and less time as new job and family obligations arise so that concerts lasting one evening are preferred to the festivals lasting several days.

---

[3] See the publication list at http://www.festivalhopper.de/festivals-2011.php.

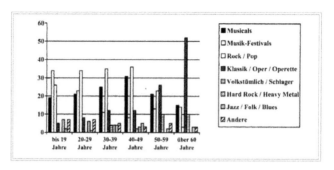

Figure 6: Share of Music Divisions in the Music Event Market in the 1st Half of 2007, Source: GfK 2007: 8.

Nowadays the motivation to attend in a festival is, due to the broad variety of festival types and music styles, a challenging research topic. Finding profound research referring to motivations why people visit a music festival is difficult, because mostly just case studies exist (see Xiang/Petrick 2006: 239 et seq.). Furthermore Lee et al point out - for festival and other events- that the most studies were done on a rural level and less on international level. The visitors' motivations would be very heterogonous, but festival manager also face the importance as a marketing tool, if the visitor groups were successful segmented (Lee et al 2003: 61). Bellinghausen moreover realized that the created atmosphere has an essential role. He underlines his opinion by the growing success of the *Jazz Festival*, even so 70 per cent of the Germans would not count this genre to its favourite music style. But especially the younger visitors of this festival mention the corporate feeling and the relaxed atmosphere as a crucial aspect for participation (see 2007: 34).

It is recognizable that SC has a great chance to reach a wide range of the society, play an important role in bringing events back to a bit more content oriented entertainment and make great contributions in the framework program. Before the options for the appropriate communication strategy are examined, music festival related sustainability challenges and measures to reverse them are the issues of the 5th part.

5. Stop Dirty Dancing - Sustainability at Music Events

It has been shown that a sustainable development needs the awakening of the consumer. Only if they move to a more efficient, consistent and sufficient life-style, would companies really care about their own performances. This might be a disadvantage for the event industry, but contains for organizers as well a great chance to set a good and promotionally effective example for improvement. Within this chapter sustainable challenges of music festivals will be presented and afterwards sustainable ambitions festival operators have already adapted.

5.1. Environmental Impact of Music Festivals and the Demand for Transition

The most popular festivals have grown so much that they get visited by an average of nearly 40,000 visitors (see table below). *Rock am Ring* had yet 85,000 visitors. An on-going trend that even established festivals keep on growing and still new festivals arise can be faced. And due to the modern communication possibilities managers are able to push established and new festivals further.

To get a feeling of the environmental impact of Germany's music festivals, the ten most popular music festivals, ranked by *openairguide.net*, are listed below. Elio Bucher, operator of this website remarked via mail that the results are influenced through the high proportion of Swiss attendees. Nevertheless, the result is based on more than 600,000 votes, so that it offers a good impression of the favoured festivals (see appendix 1). The great difference between the numbers is mainly due to the available capacity. Thus *Haldern Pop* decided to keep it small since a few decades and it is remarkable that many people seem to like this strategy (see Haldern Pop 2012). However, the amount of people, who come together just for a few days, is roughly the size of a middle sized city, but without a permanent existing infrastructure on site.

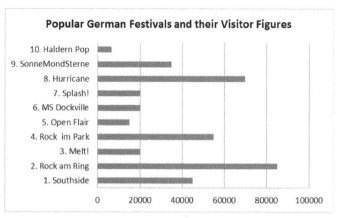

Popular German Festivals and their Visitor Figures

Figure: 7: 10 Most Popular German Festivals and their Visitor Figures Referring toOpenairguide.net; Source: Author.

The music industry in general is as a service sector not categorized as very energy or carbon intensive. Emissions occur due to energy-supply for offices, music venues or CD-manufacturing. But the picture changes, when the emissions for the, often international, travel of staff, artists and audience get included. Due to the Oxford scientists, 500 British festivals produce in total

84,000 tonnes of CO_2 every year. The most emissions are due to the audience travel with two thirds of the whole emissions.

Apart from that, diesel power generators on the festival site are the second largest polluter. Of course carbon emissions are not the only problem, but it is an established equivalent as a measure for the human impact on climate change (see Bottrill et al 2008: 49 et seq.).

Consequently, a lot of huge environmental challenges arose, which should be treated separately from the energy and transport tasks. Thus, the supply of conventional food supports the industrialized food system - with all the effects on environment, health, economy and workers' rights. Additionally, many events use materials on a large scale and with a non-renewable character so that there is a huge potential for waste reduction from the operators site.

It is not recognizable that experience-oriented offers will forgo having all the changes from event to event, and never seen before specials. Here Lucas and Matys see a crucial problem for implementing sustainability. It demands the reuse of settings, material etc., against what events typically claim a permanently change. But there is also a chance, as staging material gets scarcer as well, that it will give incentives to switch to a modest staging (see Lucas/Matys 2003: 25).

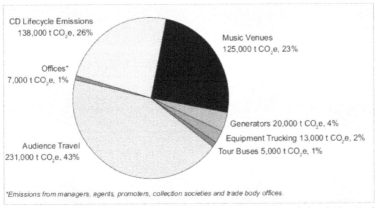

Figure 8: GHG Emissions per Annum from the UK Music Market Recorded and Live Total, GHG Emissions = ~ 540,000 t CO2e; Source: Bottrill et al 2008: 8.

Considering that the music festival is an event with its own institutional context, a lot of improvements can be achieved. Based on the work of *Green Music Initiative*, AGFA and WWFs' hints for sustainable events (see GMI, 2011; AGFA, 2012a: 2-7/ Léopold, 2011) seven working areas for sustainability management, including all three sustainability strategies, were examined and summarized in the following table. Before developing the idea of SC, the working areas should be definitely known to perform the communication strategy adequately.

Table 1: Music Festival Sustainability Management

Section	Sustainable Challenge	Events Objective
Catering	• Supporting Industrial food system harms ecosystems, • Produces vague quality • leads to high CO_2- emissions due to global transport distances	➢ Preference of local and organic food suppliers ➢ Offering more vegetarian meals ➢ Low-impact packaging and disposal ➢ Supplying fair trade products, if they are important but not available locally (like coffee) ➢ Encourage established partner to change towards a more sustainable assortment
Energy	• Energy consumption based on fossil fuels foster CO_2 emissions and therewith climate change • 'Black sheeps' among bio fuel supplier	➢ Reduction of power consumption on the festival area and along the whole supply chain ➢ Supply through on-site renewables sources like solar panels and wind mills ➢ Energy efficiency checks at the festival site and in offices ➢ Only usage of certified bio fuels ➢ Encouragement of corporation partners to check their processes for energy efficiency and to use green energy

Biodiversity	• Local habitats were affected by the festival due to the required space, waste, pollution and noise • Due to the use of unsustainable products and service fosters the event global damages of biodiversity	➢ Taking waste, resource and procurement and water management seriously ➢ Encouraging the crowd to use declared toilets and to keep the camp and festival site clean; ➢ Invitation of NGOs to campaign during the festival and to become active in the framework program ➢ Protection of local wildlife and habitats from any negative impacts ➢ Supporting creation of new habitats (as well as CO_2 stores)
Mobility	• Mobility causes the most pollution during a music festival • Beside negative climate effects does it further raise air and noise pollution	➢ Encouragement of attendees to use public transport or car sharing and charging car parking ➢ Encouragement of attendees to behave quieter outside the festival area ➢ Provide public services and set incentives for usage ➢ Efficient transportation of the festival team ➢ Supporting the planning of efficient tour routes for artists, the respective crew and equipment ➢ Investigate total carbon emissions and compensate them
Procurement and Resource Use	• Excessive and global procurement leads to high CO_2- emissions • Exploitation of resources and environmental harm • Losses for regional providers, which produce less emissions	➢ Reduction of material use where ever possible ➢ Usage of long-lasting sustainable materials, purchased preferably locally ➢ Substituting nonreturnable against reusable; ➢ Avoiding wasteful printings like flyers ➢ Encouragement of attendees and corporation partners to reduce packaging and one- way- materials
Waste Management, Re-Use and Recycling	• Discarded camping gear, packaging etc. leads to huge disposals during a festival, what harms the local environment as a waste of valuable reusable resources	➢ Offering deposit systems and careful products during the festival ➢ Encouragement of re-use, recycling and composting among attendees and suppliers ➢ Creation of energy out of waste
Water Management	• Providing the festival with fresh water is essential; but it is as well one of the most important resources, which gets soaked dramatically through festival days	➢ Usage of water efficient materials, like low-flow-shower heads and water-free toilets ➢ Advising cleaner to use water saving methods ➢ Water supply for food stalls only through central standpipes ➢ Replacing misting stations by human with hand-held water sprays ➢ Storage and recycling of grey water and avoidance of waste water pollution

Of course there is no entitlement to completeness and some parts mentioned by the sources were summarized or omitted. Thus, Léopold's point regarding *health and happiness* (see Léopold 2011) was not included as it is not directly linked to the greening of the music festivals and is therewith not in the focus of the present paper.

The need to tackle these challenges can be better understood by taking a look at the previously mentioned growth dilemma. If the festival shifts to very efficient lightning and electronic, but it is still growing so that more material is needed, the absolute energy use would very likely still grow. That does not mean that energy efficiency is worthless. It simply shows that organizers have to step up their efforts as well in consistency (e. g. providing environmental-friendly shampoo) and especially sufficiency measures (e. g. avoiding waste through reusable material) to substitute unavoidable emissions and present a convincing sustainability strategy.

It is also clear that due to such a mass event, visitors can influence the sustainability performance a lot, no matter whether looking at left camping gear, the use of the campsite as a toilet or taking the car to reach the festival. Another aspect, which at least should be mentioned, is the possibility that festival fans would evoke probably more CO_2-emissions, if they did not attend festivals. Thus, due to the importance of festivals for many groups as outlined in chapter four, it is at least conceivable that some of the attendees avoid long distance holidays in favour of specific festivals they do not want to miss. However, the visitors' part is picked up in the empirical part, where the potentials of visitor participation become investigated.

5.2. Sustainability Ambitions in the Music Festival Scene

The list of music festivals seems to be endless. Hence, it would be hard to identify ambitious representatives in an own research. Luckily already established initiatives, especially *A Greener Festival Award (see AGAF 2012b)*, the *Green Music Initiative* (see GMI 2012) and *Julie's Bicycle (see JB 2012)*, exist, which work on the greening of the music branch as a whole and of the music festivals in particular. Festival organizers are well advised to take action, as even more and more artists face the sustainability problems. Supported by the consultant Will Moore, vocalists like Jack Johnson have begun to draw up contracts, which demand to run the event sustainably. They are even allowed to cancel the performance, if the sustainability efforts do not go in line with their claims- a worst case scenario for a festival manager (see Arte 2008).

A look at the latest ranking of '*A Greener Festival Award*', which honoured 46 festivals for their sustainability efforts, reveals that no German festival has won an award (full list seen appendix 2). Of course it is possible that the festival organizers in Germany are not yet familiar with this award and it is especially known in the UK as it was founded there. But also Australia, USA, Finland, France, Sweden, Scotland, Norway, Czech Republic and even Jersey are in the list. Has the trend not yet reached the German festival operators or do they face less pressure from the festival fans?

Figure 9: Winning Nations honored by AGFA 2011; Source: Author, based on Westbury 2012.

However, the data base of the *GMI* shows that there are ambitions within the German music festival scene; especially the festivals *Melt!, Hurricane, Southside and RhEINKULTUR* showing great contributions. In January 2012, the *Melt!*-festival even won the European *GREEN'N'CLEAN Festival Award* at the Eurosonic Noorderslaag (see EFA 2012).

It is clear that festivals awarded by AGFA are not the only ones already conscious of their sustainability performance. Nevertheless, does it provide a good overview about festivals, which definitely overtake considerable efforts. They offer as well a great base to identify successful communication methods in this chapter. To categorize the festivals, the latter one was allocated for truly outstanding and inspirational events, which are the following ones (see appendix 2):

• Croissant Neuf Summer Party (England)	• Peats Ridge (Australia)
• Falls Festival, Lorne, Victoria (Australia)	• Shambala (England)
• Falls Festival, Marion Bay, Tasmania (Australia)	• Sunrise Celebration (England)
• Isle of Wight Festival (England)	• We Love Green (France)
• Lightning in a Bottle (USA)	• Wood (England)
• Oya Festival (Norway)	• Woodford Festival (Australia)

These need to be exceptional events, which have "significantly reduced greenhouse gas emissions, have excellent travel, transport and waste management programs, protect the environment and minimize water use and communicate this to the public", (AGFA, 2011: 4).

The Glastonbury Festival reached the lower status of 'highly commended' and the Roskilde Festival takes part but was not awarded, but both strongly approach sustainability communication, as examined by Meegan Jones (2009) so that they provide as well an interesting research input.

6.   Realizing Sustainability Communication

This chapter includes firstly the arguments for music festival operators to consider sustainability communication and comprises furthermore the demands of SC according to customers as well as for other stakeholders groups, which are additional important multipliers of the message.

It shows further successful implemented measures of festival operators and how the sustainability communication influences the overall sustainability performance remarkably.

6.1.   Incentives for and Demands on the Festival Operators

Apparently, many festivals worldwide have already begun to take responsibility. That this is profitable for the society and for operators, due to cost reductions within the operation of the event, is quite clear. But it is as well interesting for income aspects. O'Neill publishes that festival managers adjust to the trends that customers are conscious of sustainability topics. Indeed, due to an earlier research, believe 36 per cent that the festivals environmental credential would have a

huge or definite influence of the customers' decision for their ticket purchase (O'Neill 2009: 22).

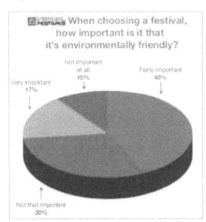

It is likely that festival goers in Germany would answer this question similarly. However, it is an issue to look at in the empirical part.

Hence, it is also conceivable that the conscious and confident implementing of sustainability elements in events, even in the framework program, could be the right substitute and counterpart against the overloaded offers explained earlier. This approach can rest upon the newly arisen wave of participation in eco-friendly projects, especially beyond the younger generation. Therefore two essential points can be identified.

Figure 10: Importance of Festivals Environmentalism for Visitors, Source: O'Neills 2009: 21.

First, people do have a strong connection to nature and environmentalism is relevant for them, no matter whether they can grasp or want to ignore their own responsibility (see BMU, 2010: 35). The on-going pollution has reached a societal recognized critical point that has also animated opinion leaders to espouse public awareness (see Bieber 2007).

Second, the rapid development and application of the earlier mentioned social media enables groups and individuals to share information and to find proponents easily, so that a wider, strengthening support for sustainability issues can be realized (see Rheinländer et al 2011: 95 et seq.).

In the context of event marketing and live communication, the third chapter has examined that marketing communication instruments can be used for the cultivation of sustainability, even if there is the risk that its core value could be reduced to fit in an entertainment format (see Lucas/Matys 2003: 16).

Nevertheless, many participants of music festivals are part of the described group, who do not care deliberately about the festivals' sustainability issues and they would not be the first addressees for content issues. But this is the literal challenge: Reaching a non-involved group and making them behaving more sustainably through sustainability communication measures.

Therefore, Lucas and Wilts also say, that to touch the participant emotionally it is necessary to let them participate in the program. For the realization of such campaigns, examples of the live communication have shown that it is helpful to partner with different organizations to use already established skills. That offers new chances for sustainable market segmentation, but demands undeniably an opening on the part of the operators. However, Lucas and Wilts see as well a need for clarification regarding the possible staging potential of sustainability during an event (Lucas/Wilts 2004: 44 et seq.).

Bowdin et al and Yoeman et al say that events are a way to reach the public and influence attitudes. Especially because the event branch reaches a high range of direct consumers so that a smart sustainability strategy, assuming it is well communicated, could probably transport the message of sustainability consumption to a much higher degree and more comprehensively than other branches (see Bowdin et al 2010: 170 et seq. and Yoeman et al 1999). Bowdin et al state:

"The environmentally conscious event manager will reap not only economic benefits, but also the approval of an increasingly environmentally aware public", (Bowdin et al 2010: 172).

Due to the rising importance of sustainability in public, the consistent implementation of creative sustainability communication integrated in the framework program improves the image of the event branch as well. There is a quite high potential that the direct as well as indirect sustainability measures will find great support of the participants and can overtake an essential part in the events' image building communication strategy. Lucas and Wilts see even business opportunities for events arranged for sustainability itself (see Lucas/Wilts, 2004).

If it succeeds in reaching these people, verifiable by *Key Performance Indicators* (KPIs), less CO_2-emissions or less waste and so on occur during the festival. Surveys after the festival could register an increase in prestige and could praise for having a positive impact regarding a cultural change and boosting the idea of sustainability within society. This would rather lead to an indirect compensation of the festivals emissions. Indeed, it is hard to prove, how strongly people become influenced. But assuming they would take some ideas for self-determination at home and caring afterwards a little more for consumption, waste production, eating and mobility habits, the event could be much more successful in sustainability issues, than just improving the sustainability performing behind the scenes.

Nevertheless, to avoid the reduction of sustainability aspects to an enjoyable format, as considered by Lucas et al, manager must implement reliable sustainability measures and be reliable in their communication.

Various examples, emerging on the following pages, demonstrate that this can be successful and works out pretty well. It is detectable that they mostly combine strong efforts to improve their own sustainability performance with an offensive communication strategy transporting the message of sustainability. Therefore, they work not only on making sustainability issues interesting for the festival attendees, but also use the aspiration after the recognition of the individual in its peer group. As mentioned in chapter four, the corporate feeling is one of the most important things to participate in a music festival (see p. 24). If crew and actors transport the message that sustainability is an important issue, among the festival community, it potentially nudges the participants to adapt the sustainable lifestyle meaning, too.

Facing that SC is an important part of the event management, it should be considered carefully and fitting to the specific stakeholders. Thus, the respective issues get presented corresponding to the specific target group.

6.2.   Green Message – Subtle or Slather

To transport the green message a lot of measures are possible. This could be for instance a mass tree planting campaign instead of a motocross show or a common bicycle-powered-energy initiative instead of a firework. Whatever, the management has still to keep in mind, how far they can go. Greening the festival is great and should be done, but pushing the whole one too intensely into the eco-movement could spoil the festival's image and scare many fans away (see Jones 2009: 38). Finding the right balance between offering decent sustainability education and fun is the crunch-point regarding the entertainment program and can be a really enrichment of the whole event as the way of communication depends very much on the attendees attitudes and values (see Lucas 2007: 54).

It is very likely that most of the team members, attendees and partner will appreciate the efforts for a greener festival, but are nevertheless not interested in starting a new hippy-movement. Thus what is possible and what might destroy the festival image and vibe should be carefully examined in advance.

That means: Greening either way, but communication fitting to the crowd and to the general festival design.

Hence, regarding the framework program, it is helpful to directly ask the crowd what is interesting for them. Further important counterparts are the front-line crew interacting with the attendees and knowing the needs best. Another point to mention is that within the communication with any stakeholder group, the truth should not be overstretched. Laying it on thickly might be great for the image as long as nobody does closer research. If somebody discovers that the representation of measures is exaggerated it is not far away from getting postmarked for green washing (see Jones 2009: 38 et seq.).

Many festivals put their green activities among one label so that the topic can be treated separately from other information. Focus a green theme through all operations and within the event's program is an option to kick-start the greening, asking content programmers to bring sustainability themes into their parts. This was done at the Glastonbury Festival in 2007, where they run the 'Stop Climate Chaos – I count'- Campaign, encouraging attendees to get involved and to change their private behaviour (see Oxfam 2011).

Once again: It is most important to be convincing regarding the direct sustainability measures and to communicate them in the right manner. Considering this, a subtle strategy could be more convincing than an exaggerated eco-event program.

6.3. Communication with the Involvement of Staff and Corporation Partners

The focus lays on the SC strategy for festival visitors. The current part summarizes issues for SC regarding important stakeholders like staff or corporation partners, as they are, already mentioned earlier, important multipliers for the sustainability message.

Convincing the Crew

Due to the interdisciplinary sustainability does affect pretty well every part of the event organization. Due to that, Jones advises to never forget to motivate the team that will need to be on board. They need to be briefed regarding the single sustainability issues. However, what is true for the attendees, it does also count for the involved team and members of partnering businesses. This means that even if some participants are enthusiastic to support the greening of the festival, the idea still needs to be sold to others. If this point is ignored, some helpful additional input could be lost and even the final success could be affected (see Jones 2009: 45 et seq.).

If all experts of the individual sections understand the relevance of the topic and want to get involved in the greening of the music festival, solutions can be found earlier, easier and to the utmost satisfaction. And undoubtedly, dedicated staff-members are more able to inspire the visitors of the festival than those who are not.

The intension to talk out the efforts done and planned is necessary and helpful, but it also matters how the information is transmitted. To keep the stakeholder in line the following communication methods are advisable (see Jones 2010: 57):

- Sustainability briefings and meetings, where stakeholder-ideas and contribution are considered;
- Integration of stakeholders ad-hoc-ideas and decisions;
- Integration of sustainability themes in the regular meetings.

It is vital to create a special resource website for staff and contractors to post requirements and gain information about status quo of the sustainability measures as well as about additional material for the own improvement, e. g. guidelines for sustainable printing or energy use. This should also include regular reports to update and make improvement suggestions for concerned parties, possibly by sending newsletters explaining advantages of specific issues. A good example is the additional website of the *Festival Republic*, called *Green Republic*, which also sends out regularly a newsletter for stakeholders (see GR 2010).

The information should not stop during the festival days. The most staff members and volunteers supporting the event have not been involved before. That needs the transfer of the information and the excitement for sustainability through briefing-sessions, hand-outs and posters visible in the staff headquarter. They should be well informed on what is done to run this event sustainably to be motivated, to consider this in their tasks and to inform curious visitors (see Jones 2010: 58 et seq.)

Sponsors and Partners

Sponsoring is as well an important communication tool, where the sponsor as an external stakeholder and the event organizer aid one another, recognizable, for instance, with a look at the combination of the energy drink *Red Bull* and extreme sport events like Formula 1 or Base Jumping. This led finally in 2010 to the winning of the *Sport business Award* (see Mortsiefer 2010).

Thus, during the selection of a sponsoring partner attention should be paid to the sustainability approaches of the potential partner to underline the events' sustainable attitude. This must not be natural muesli with reduced protein content, but however, getting support from a roadster producer is not the best starting point from which to talk about sustainability. Likewise, the *RheinKultur* Festival is sponsored by green electricity provider *Naturwatt* (see RK 2011).

It is also advisable that sponsoring further regards the preferability of regional businesses instead of one perceived green big player from the other side of the globe.

The sponsor earns from this cooperation an upgrading of their image beyond the mostly younger music fans. So, a green sponsor could nudge the audience to consider the topic, for instance renewable energy, and the audience recognizes the sponsor as part of their beloved music festival (see Thaler/Sandstein 2009: 24 et seq.).

Neco, a store for sustainable living, sponsors for instance two biodiesel run vans for a festival. Another option is to ask natural cosmetic producer to provide shower creme for free (Jones 2009: 49 et seq.). Also plausible are special offers for a train shuttle service or a discount on the purchase in a partnering bio supermarket, when showing the ticket.

It is as well possible to invite established NGOs for the presentation of a sustainability topic by creating a part of the framework program. They are normally eager for opportunities to promote their mission, know how to transport it and mobilize their own volunteers so that the organizer can outsource this task. The Glastonbury Festival is very ambitious, giving *Greenpeace* a whole area, called the *Greenpeace Field*, for their activities (see GFa 2011).

Arrangements with the Traders

Sustainability efforts should also be enforced by arrangements with the traders. So, by seeking a greener catering at the festivals, realistic targets are crucial. The Australian *Peatsridge Festival* tried to require a change of their traders to organic and ideally local food immediately. But they needed to face that this needs time and work. Meanwhile they set the goal to be 100 % organic with all food on the festival site for 2012, employ an organic food-coordinator, who is assisting the stalls with the change, and stall manager, who can be asked for further advices and supplier contacts to become organic (see PF 2011). Hence, operators should work hand in hand with the stall holders.

Unfortunately, the experiences from the catering business *GastroBüro* show that established food provider have a pretty low interest in changing their habits. Against that the new and alternative organic ones are really interested in taking part (see GMI 2011).

Reasons for the hesitance of established ones could be for instance, doubting the reliable supply of organic food or higher costs for these products. Against what Wichmann and Lucas show the saving potentials of organic food. They demonstrate that measures like less meat and usage of regional products, but also the re-use of used materials could lead to cost reductions in the supply chain (see Wichmann/Lucas 2005: 32 et seq.).

But Ströll, head of the soccer stadium Augsburg and part of the *DFB*, which works on a more sustainable event performance as well, does not believe that their customers would be willing to pay more for organic food. Until now only single instances have been changed, like organic sausages during the finale of the woman soccer championship (see Hamm/Jerger 2011: 12 et seq.).

Once convinced by sustainability efforts, traders should be encouraged to careful select the offered non-food-products and choose regional, eco-friendly or fair traded products.

There is also a huge demand in communication about waste management. So it is better to talk in front about the allowed packaging and other materials and also to be keen to encourage them to integrate or continuously advance a thorough sustainability management into their businesses like greening the office, energy and so on. Regarding their energy demand on the festival site, it is helpful to set an upper limit of available energy, like 10 amp (see Jones 2010: 51).

The Glastonbury Festival found a smart way to encourage their traders towards a green behaviour. They assigned, together with *Greenpeace* and other NGOs, the *'Green Trader Award'*, given to those traders who pushed themselves to lower the environmental impact of their businesses. With an audit scheme, improvement can be recognized and motivation will rise to reach higher measurable goals. Winner teams and pictures of them become awarded during the festival and are publicised on the festival webpage, what means a motivating appreciation for the efforts and of course a great advertisement for the awarded businesses (see GF 2011b). The same idea is used at the *Shambala Festival* (see SF 2011).

Local Authorities

Communication about the festivals by working together with local authorities offers probably great solutions to participate in already established sustainability program, which can be adapted during the festival. Probably the region has a branded recycling campaign, which is transferable. This is as well an opportunity to show good will and to generate a broader acceptance of the festival in the region (see Jones 2010: 52).

Power Supplier

Corporations with a company offering clean energy solutions like wind generators, eco-paint supplier or zero energy products like solar power phone chargers, ideally located in the region, would be a chance to present their clean energy solutions to the young community. As seen at the festival location Ferropolis in Saxony Anhalt, where through the corporation of *Ferropolis GmbH, Melt! Festival* and the photovoltaic company *Q-cells* a solar system was installed, running since June 2011. It generates 189.000 kWh per year and therewith two and a half times more than the *Melt!* Festival needs (see DGAP-Media 2011).

Generic for the outdoor events is the usage of mobile power generators, which normally work through pollutive mineral diesel. Meanwhile, power biodiesel-using generators, made from waste vegetable oil, and also mobile solar power generators exist, which have the same power and reliability like diesel units (see e. g. www.solarover.com).

To reach a modest deployment of generators an accurate planning for their placements, size, loads and usage peaks et cetera is needed. The charged power contractors are the experts in this field. Offering a bonus for less generator use could be an incentive, but the other way around also involves the risk of too little energy. Hence, a festival sustainability manager equipped with the basic education in power supply helps to figure out the optimum demand and avoids mistrust. Once distributed, it is as well important to name responsible persons checking the phases, when non-solar generators do not need to run. There should also be kept an eye on possible overstating of power demands on behalf of the production staff (Jones 2009: 86 et seq.).

Involvement of the Artists

Artists are the important role models, who can bring the transportation of sustainability issues to real success. As opinion leaders they have a high influence, not only in setting fashion trends, and can greatly support the festivals targets (see Lazarsfeld et al 1968: 49 et seq.). Many of well-known singers are already engaged for climate protection or environmentalism and would likely love to support campaigns for sustainability. This became obvious through the *Live Earth* concert in 2007, were 150 music stars performed for the avoidance of CO_2. Some musicians let offset their CO_2 emissions arising by their touring, in Germany for example *Peter Fox, Jan Delay* or the band *Juli* as well as international stars like *Kelly Clarckson* or the band *Radiohead* (see Colin 2011: 7 et seq.).

Hence, asking convinced artists to participate in the event makes things much easier. But also not obvious engaged artists should be asked. Maybe they already have in mind that it is time for them to participate or just like to present themselves as caring individuals.

The application possibilities are various. Tackling the themes in their performance brings great attention to the sustainability challenges.

Megan Jones writes concerning this matter:

> "Through songs, performance, theatre and art potent statements can be made on environmental and social issues. They can entice and empower crowds of people to take on issues, and with collective action invoke change." (Jones 2009: 52-53).

Thus, they could as well function as spokesperson for a specific topic or support an NGO- campaign on the festivals campsite. Of course, the limits of participation need to be considered. A famous singer cannot just walk across the campsite without getting overrun. Creating a prize competition among the bus or train takers could be an appropriate alternative.

Here is definitely a great chance to involve the artists pre-event as well as during the festival, and further to switch from a very loud, expensive, spectacular framework program to visitors-integrating, visionary and eco-friendly offerings.

Pushing Building Owner

Sustainable buildings are barely used, during a music festival. However, they were needed to provide water toilets and sleeping facilities for the artists.

Regarding established and not newly planned festivals operators face fixed conditions. As the buildings normally not owned by the festival organizers, the building administration can be advised to use green electricity, energy saving lamps and to start remediation measures. According to this should a national accreditation scheme for renewable energies kept in mind, which helps to avoid bad publicity due to the green washing of the energy supplier (see Jones 2010: 80).

In case that a completely new festival is planned or the location should be changed than the organizers can avoid the readjustment by carefully selecting a venue, which is already eco-friendly. Nevertheless, it is great, if sustainable materials were even considered during the construction, but it should be kept in mind that new buildings also do contribute to an additional land consumption, which is a huge problem, especially in Germany (see Lucas 2008: 411 et seq.). That means that refurbished residential buildings should be preferred.

Miscellaneous Stakeholder

Further stakeholder groups, which at least should be named, are the venue owner, the media, the local community and probable industry associations, which must be informed in an honest and transparent manner about the sustainability goals to get their support (see Jones 2010: 53 et seq.).

However, corporation partners and the crew afford the advantage that they can be convinced easier as a *B2B* relationship exists and the festival is an important income source for them. Indeed, partner could be selected, which can identify with the vision of greening the event. The task to reach attendees, which come to have a good time, to relax and therefore pay a lot, is much more difficult.

6.4.   Communication with Attendees

The correct deployment of the communication tools in front of and during the event is crucial for a successful realization of sustainability goals. Many festivals have already developed great ideas about how to change the behaviour of the crowd. The previous pages show, how a fun-seeking audience can be reached respective to the different phases.

6.4.1. In Advance Festival Communication

As described earlier, at least some attendees do look for festivals, which consider sustainability issues. To catch the others as well and as some measures need preparation, it is essential to promote the efforts in advance.

Determination and Realization of Communication Policy

As the Internet is meanwhile the most important information source for the purchase decisions in general, especially among the young generation, it is the most important communication methods for organizers (see Shahd/Pols 2010). Thus, communication in front of the festival needs mostly the modern instruments like the festival website, newsletters and of course the social media tools like *facebook* (see p. 13). With it, they could transport all the sustainability themes addressed to the attendees.

Due to the previous characterization of the festival fans, the focus should be laid to the suggestive (emotional) effect of the advertisement to obtain the broad mass (see p. 15). Nevertheless, detailed information should be reachable via further links for the interested reader. The time frame for the information should be selected carefully. For instance researches found out that visitors arrange on average three week prior to the festival how they will arrive; some of course earlier. Hence, all mobility offers on behalf of the operator should be fixed much earlier than this and be promoted powerfully around this time (see Jones 2010: 64).

Festivals' Sustainability Efforts

To make the activities work, it is essential to promote the respective information through event promotions, any websites and other advertising efforts. If the greening of the festival has gotten a green theme with a specific name or brand for the activities, it makes sense to put all relevant information under this title as made by many festivals. For instance the *Falls Festival* collects their information beyond the typical 'sustainability' term (see FF 2011a). Others linked their efforts to the festival name like the *Melt!*- Festival, where the item '*M!ECO*' can be found in the menu bar of the website (see *Melt!* 2011a). It is also possible to set a leading campaign on the homepage, as done by Glastonbury with the '*love the farm – leave no trace*' – campaign (see GF 2011c).

However, the websites' sustainability part should give an overview about how sustainability themes were tackled, what has already been realized (using key indicators) and which planned goals must be reached. Furthermore it should include what behaviour the organizers expect from the audience during their stay to minimize the environmental pollution. Glastonbury Festival realized this by putting the sustainability issues beyond the topic '*Green Glastonbury*', divided in '*What we do*' and '*What you can do*'. In the last part they set just simple hints like '*use the butt bins*' and '*do not waste water*' with a short note why this hint is so important (see GF 2011d). For instance:

USE THE 'BUTT BINS'. Please use the big white cigarette bins around the site. A cigarette butt can take up to 8 years to break down. There will also be buckets of sand outside venues to put your cigarettes out, please use them.

Figure 11: Communication Example Making a Sustainable Problem Tangible for Festival Fans; Source Glastonbury 2011d.

From the communication perspective it is remarkably that they use the KISS- principle, what means to *keep it short and simple*. The sentence behind the hint affects the smoker, as it is not formulated as an accusation, rather as an interesting piece of information about which long-term effects arose by this subsidiary action. Clear indications are rather able to reach people (see Seufert 2010: 32).

This is also the experience of sustainability manager Jones as an employee of a production company. Who she was working with explained to her that he was shocked as he found out through a telecast that it needs 400 years for a plastic bottle to break down (see Jones 2010: 47). She wondered afterwards: *"Even though I'd been talking to him about recycling every day for a month, the penny had finally dropped for him and we went on to make some great waste plans"*, (Jones 2010: 47).

To inform *Melt!*-festival attendees about basic sustainability issues, the German climate campaign *'Klima sucht Schutz'* composes a target-group-specific guide for climate friendly behaviour during the festival, online as free download available in A4 format, designed in a youth style to interfold it in pocket format. So, with picking up their attendees needs (attractiveness, recognition, belonging) in a casual manner, they even involve topics like giving up shaving the bear and blow-drying the hair during the festival as nice guys would not play rock'n' roll and the hair is looking forward to dry in the wind (see appendix 3, German edition).

Ticket Purchase

With the purchase of the ticket it is clear that the person definitely wants to come to the festival. Once at this point can he or she be nudged to do a good deed. Thus, the *Splendour in the Grass* offers on a voluntarily basis to offset the average carbon emissions over a 48-hours period with the purchase of a Green Ticket for 7 dollar. The money is spent on renewable energy projects. Nearly one quarter purchased such a ticket (see Jones 2010: 124 et seq.).

Another option is to sell festival tickets in combination with a discounted train or bus ticket, which is discussed in the following mobility part.

Mobility

For the big challenge, the reduction of festival-caused emissions; the festival manager must offer alternatives to private driving, which advantages are outstanding for the attendees. Thus, alternatives need to be promoted to be more attractive than car-driving. That means to offer on the one hand alternatives for the reasons, which drive the persons to use a car, and to set incentives above, so that it is probably even more fun or more comfortable to take the provided coaches or trains.

For instance GF promotes the bus shuttle service of the corporation partner *National Express* as one of the best ways to get there and with the argument that the shuttle stops right in front of the entrance. Against this option, arriving by car to Glastonbury means 25 dollar parking fee (see GF 2011e). Due to the different car parks, which become filled in a different speed, they let visitors know that *"[i]t is really down to luck whereabouts in the car park you end up"*, (GF 2011f). This displays how strongly organizer can influence the attractiveness of the transport method.

Figure 12: Advertisement for Glastonbury Festivals Shuttle Service; Source Glastonbury 2011e.

Nevertheless, it makes no sense, if most of the audience needs to go to work the next day and the first bus starts in the late evening. Providing shuttle services demands an adequate planning to make this experience a good one. It is useful to combine it with a special combi-ticket for train/coach and festival, whereby people can save money and find enough space for all the stuff they carry to the event. A broad campaign was introduced by the *Melt!*-festival in 2010. Thereby, their main communication argument has been environmental pollution and their ambitions to reduce their impact so that they encourage their attendees to avoid car use and offering them a *Festival-Hotelzug* (transl. hotel train). They further promote the offer of a coach shuttle service and reached that *Deutsche Bahn* provides a special ticket for *Melt!*-attendees, usable in every train for a fixed price of 79 Euro (see *Melt!* 2011b).

Furthermore, if posting information about the festivals mobility offers at the website, it should be made together with a message, that camping gear can be hired at the festival. This reduces the weight of the luggage and avoids another shopping tour for camping gear, what gives pleasure to the attendee and the sustainability goals. The loose of flexibility by arriving via train or by bus is the next challenges, which demands of course a reliable and regular shuttle services to be properly convincing.

However, not everybody can be convinced to take the public transport system. Indeed, it is not necessary, if people arrive in a full car. Due to a DEFRA Report carpooling would generate even less CO_2 than traveling by train. The *Big Chill* Festival publishes this information on the website and promotes therewith their sustainable travel solutions, including their own *goCarShare* campaign. On a separate *facebook*-connected website festival attendees can easily find drivers or car passengers (see BCF 2011).

The *Coachella Festival* has in cooperation with the NGO *Global Inheritance* introduced in 2007 the *CARPOOLCHELLA* program, where VIP tickets or *'Coachella for life'*-vouchers and other prices can be won. The experience of the last years has shown that this has been well received by the attendees. As cars, which obviously taking part in the program (visible CARPOOLCHELLA inscription), get selected during the festival, the attendees develop creative ideas to get attention in the selection process, what is of course an additional promotion program for the idea behind (see CF 2011).

Hence, there are many options to promote a more sustainable travelling, which just need a bit of creativity and a good management.

Procurement, Resource Use and Waste Avoidance

In preparation for the festival, attendees purchase much food and non-food items. The packaging usually is left as waste at the festival site. Encouraging a more sustainable consumption can help to reduce this amount.

Firstly, it is useful to strongly promote discount opportunities of cooperation partners, which offer sustainable product solutions like a solar light bulb or organic food. For instance corporates *Vermont Brewers' Festival* with the NGO *Food and Water Watch* to distribute Burlington tap water at the festival. Attendees could get a fill-up of their glass, canteen, or whatever for free and as often they want (see Schuetz 2009). The distribution of the message that water is available for free is the best prevention for water bottle slathers. The *Lightning in a Bottle Festival* prevents as well fresh water for free and encourages the visitors to bring their own bottle and to bring even own dishes and cutlery, what can be used when food gets bought (see LiB 2011a). If furthermore a natural cosmetic producer sponsors shower crème and shampoo, it should as well be communicated in advance. On the one hand it is an additional advertisement what satisfies the partners and on the other hand some people would avoid buying extra toiletries, if they know it is available for free.

Camping gear is as well a famous for being left at the campsite, what can be avoided by similar campaigns. So the *'love your tent'*-campaign, developed by the *Isle of Wight Festival* (IoWF) and corporation partners, calls attention for carrying home camping gear for reuse after the event is over. They inform on their website that it takes 485 man-hours to remove only the camping gear and that it costs money which could be better used for entertainment at the festival (see IoWF 2011).

Beside the encouragement, it is possible to arrange donation points, where attendees can hand in their tents and inform themselves in front of the festival at the website why and what will be done with it. Jones writes according to this topic as they get the task to encourage the audience handing in their camping gear at UK festivals:

> *"We ended up with 10,000 items of camping gear donated, and were actually quite overwhelmed by it all (...). I would prefer them to take their gear home and re-use it, but we are talking about kids that tend to prefer to blow tents up (yes, like bomb, not an air mattress) at the end of the festival, so handing them in is quite a massive achievement"*, (see Jones 2010: 62).

In order to avoid further attendees waste, festivals corporate with businesses, which rent camping gear so that music fans arrive at the festival and their camping ground is already prepared. This has already picked up in Germany realized by the service *Mein Zelt steht schon* and was available at more than 20 festivals in the season 2012/2013. Attendees can book online tents plus chairs and so on. No hands turn is needed, as the set up service is included (http://www.mein-zelt-steht-schon.de/).

Last but not least should be named a simple but clever idea from a festival what has not set an obvious SC at their website. However, the idea of *MS Dockville* (MSD) managers to open a festival supermarket and to publish a price list of the favoured goods on their webpage goes in this direction. Fans of the festival can look up the prices online, realizing that they are feasible and no extensive purchase is necessary. Indeed, they have no incentives to buy food in advance, when they can get it there – fresh and refrigerated. Another real sustainable approach has been made by *MS Dockville*, which describes itself as art and music festival: it offers the *'Freihandelszone'*, a free trade zone in its pure meaning, as attendees are invoked at the website to sign as a trader of self-made, up- and recycled products at the festival (see MSD 2011). Hence, as the festival concept seems to work out well it is a good example for the mentioned indirect SC, supporting sustainable development, without naming it. Nevertheless, without informing their fans somewhere about the sustainable impact, they give away the opportunity to profile themselves by the sustainability aware audience.

Announcing Sustainability in the Framework Program

The last topic to be outlined is the need for promoting a special framework program to emphasize sustainability issues. The *Croissant Neuf Summer Party* (CN), winner of the *'Greener Festival Award'*, has made an environmental-friendly and interactive framework program to its trade mark. Hence, instead of firework or stunt-shows, they entertain their participants with an eclectic frame workshop program from dancing to Windmill making or Woodland crafts – which can be looked up in advance (see CN 2011). Those add-ons in the program have the effect to bring people closer to issues regarding nature without being obtrusive. Some festivals go beyond this an invite NGOs to take part and spread their message. This could be tough in way, as promotion activities often considered annoying like in pedestrian areas, where NGOs call for donations (see Martens 2011). Thus, information in advance about the NGO their goals and the reasons why the festival operators are keen to let them take part are helpful to obtain acceptance and arouse curiosity beyond the attendees. That ones who already have an interest in the topic, get the change to collect some information in advance and so are probably inspired to arrange their contribution possibilities at the festival together with the NGO. So, LiB enthusiastically promotes the invited NGOs and their projects on their website (see LiB 2011b). At GF the participation of their charity partners is an established part of the whole event. They divide the festival in different areas. One of them is called *The Green Fields* what they promote on their website as:

> *"...the soul of Glastonbury Festival, where traditional skills and new ways of thinking combine in an explosion of creativity (...). With its skyline filled with peace flags, gently turning wind generators and the outlines of dozens of tipis, this is a place to discover that there are other ways to make the world turn round other than competing and consuming"*, (GF 2011a).

Greenpeace even get their own *Greenpeace Field* and a stage, where artist performances take place. Beside detailed information about what is going on at the *Greenfields* on the website, they regularly inform fans and interested parties about news of their main charity partners *Greenpeace*, *Oxfam* and *Water Aid* on their official *facebook* account, which has more than 230,000 fans (see FB 2012a). This shows that sustainability communications can be implemented as an integral part of the festival and that it can appear sympathetic rather than quirky. However, environmentalism is part of GF from its beginnings and newbies in this field should make up their mind how strong they want to highlight it.

6.4.2. On-Festival Communication

Any information in advance does not count, when the communication at the festival gets neglected. The task it to nudge, to motivate and to show that it is worth and that it feels good to behave more sustainably. Some organizers have done a great job in this area. The following points are structured as in the sections of sustainability management in table 1 (see p. 27).

Biodiversity Climate Change

As already noted in table 1, biodiversity comprises the solution at the festival terrain as well as the treatment of biodiversity loss. The first one demands to ask the crowd for a cautious behaviour at the festival, which partially overlaps with the following sections. So, the focus here is laid on the possible educational campaigns regarding climate change, for instance education measures for CO_2-footprint reduction, or for biodiversity like nature and species conservation. If the audience understand that things like reforestation are also an important contribution to tackle climate change and that climate protection helps to save biodiversity, both issues can become tied together and festival fans interested in the one or in the other topic can be satisfied.

Once, an NGO is invited and the organizers enabled them to become creative, they can provide an additional entertainment part for the festival with a good sense behind. The picture below is one result of the *Greenpeace* campaign in 2010, where they talked with visitors of various festivals about deforestation and palm oil issues. More than 3,000 people signed up as *Forest Defenders* and 1,300 photos were taken from attendees in the 'picture frame' with the background of a *Jungle Book* canvas art worked by *Banksy* (see GP 2010).

Figure 13: *Greenpeace* **Putting Festival Fans in a Picture, Source: GP 2010.**

A very regionally focused festival, the *Green Village Music & Arts Festival*, sets as well a green area, called *Eco village*, what has a special line-up. During the festival were hold several lectures regarding a more environmental friendly lifestyle, which also includes parts as energy saving potentials (see GV 2011). Setting an individual area for those issues ensures that anybody who does not like to deal with the issues during the festival does not get bothered, but enthusiastic or curious people can just come along.

In addition, some of their music artists could take part in the initiative by at least supporting the promotion of activities in advance, even done so by the UNEPs World Environment Day Challenge, which was nominated for *'Best Green Cross Platform Digital Media Solution'* (see UNEP 2011). Artists with not such a high publicity could probably be part of a campaign and help to entertain the participants.

Sale of Goods

If the caterer have integrated organic food and have improved their sustainability performance, the crowd should be informed about it. It is helpful to develop a corporate design for the food stalls selling organic food so that orientation is easy for the hungry crowd (see GMI 2011).

Thereby, it is part of the following research, how apparently some information should be placed, for instance according to bio or fair trade labels or the information that the producer is a regional one.

The trend for bio-food is still a new one. A few years ago it was still proscribed to pay more than necessary for groceries, but food scandals and more detailed information changed the public opinion slightly (see Stockrahm 2011). So write Leitzmann et al that organic food has a rather positive image among the young generation in the age of 16 to 29. The muesli image would not be distinctive. Nevertheless, they would buy organic seldom due to higher prices and as they care less for nutrition issues. They further state that this target group does not know much about the existing labels, and are a bit more interested in the taste of the food than in environmental or social issues when making the purchase decision, even if love for animals is remarkable (see Leitzmann et al. 2009: 12).

By promoting organic food successfully during the music festival, it could raise the awareness for organic food as well a stronger self-confidence among festival visitors, who feel normally out of the ordinary, if they eat bio, vegetarian or even vegan.

An appealing tagline could convince even people, which did not care about bio-food. An example comes from the Glastonbury Festival: With a collage they demonstrated the carbon footprint of the everyday bought food. With the tangible comparison *"one basket of imported food creates more CO_2 than 6 month cooking"*, (see Jones 2010: 250), the deep impact of global food chains gets demonstrated, incidentally without long explanations. Beyond this plate is a smaller one, presenting the alternative in four words: *'buy local, organic food'* (see Jones 2010: 250). Similar presentation can be adapted for non-food products due to fair trade.

In case the festival adapted a competition to honour stall holders, which work hard to improve their sustainability performance, it would be a waste for SC to make things secret. Even though it is not set as a main stage event, would the public awarding call attention for what can and what needs to be done to run those stalls sustainably. It is further a great opportunity to raise awareness for the hard working stall holders, which would get rewarded additionally by the applause from the crowd.

Energy

Running a festival offers great opportunities for avoiding and reducing energy. Those measures are as well obviously for the participants and thus suitable for demonstrating a change towards sustainability (see Jones 2010: 78). The most important part is of course the powering of the festival by renewable energy resources. In addition initiatives help to raise the awareness for the energy problem. Hence, no matter what is installed, whether the festival offers solar heated showers, generators or wind powered stalls, there should be information boards, who tell the audience that renewable energy is used and probably how much carbon emissions will be reduced thereto so that the visitors can get a feeling for energy demands. If a partner is responsible for the provision, things become easier as the company has its strong own interest that people recognize the service. Some providers have solar and wind powered showers facilities and advertise its renewable energy products during the festival as *Navitron* at the *Big Green Gathering* (see Navitron 2007).

Figure 14: *Navitron* Showers at BGG, Source Navitron 2007.

With volunteers or corporation partners it is possible to install even energy generating bikes, where attendees can battle against each other or win something when a specific amount of energy is achieved. Participants at the *Big Green Gathering* had for instance the possibility to make their own juice by pedal power (see Jones 2010: 102-103).

Mobility

The transport issues were already solved in advance. Nevertheless, public transport and bikes should be provided and the transport efforts communicated to raise awareness beyond the crowd. The GF shows an example for additional information about the CO_2- impact of individual transport to the festival at its *Green Way*. The picture encourages all car drivers to give their cars a rest (see Jones 2010: 151).

If the festival provides a shuttle service to the next supermarket during the festival, the bus station should be at a central point, clearly signed and visible for everybody. As mentioned does it make sense to provide a phone number or info point employees can give all information about when the shuttle service is driving. When the festival area is a huge one, two or more pick up points are advisable to be convenient for the festival goers.

Waste management

Waste management demands powerful communication activities, as the participation of the crowd is crucial for success. Assuming that through the pre-communication process some waste could be avoided, still a lot will arise. However, a waste bin station cannot be positioned beside every tent. Instead, the visitors can get a set of bin bags coloured according to the waste separation system. The right timing is essential. Confronting the people arriving at the entrance is not advisable. Whilst sitting relaxed in their camping area with the first bits of rubbish requiring a bin bag will be seen rather as a useful additional service (see Jones 2010: 337).

One small thing makes a lot of trouble: a cigarette butt. Festival goers smoke a lot. Beside the additional carbon emissions the butts are a tough waste problem and very harmful for the local environment.

Hence, beside well-signed ashtrays, there are personal ashtrays, which provide a great advertising space for sponsoring partner or the festival itself. There could also be used the opportunity for personalization to increase their usage likability. Festivals are a great chance to distribute this product. Once the critical mass is achieved, they would become probably as usual as lighter and cigarette box for smokers.

Figure 15: Peats Ridge Festival also Designed a Noticeable Waste Location; Source: Yusaf, P.

So, *Southbound Festival* offers smokers personal ashtrays for free (see Jones 2010: 339). For some it might be a nice particular souvenir as well.

Another reason for waste is the serving material used by the food stall holders. Adding a deposit on bottles or cans is a proven way to avoid waste where it rises, as it is an incentive to hand the drinking vessel in. Otherwise the individual obtains a welfare loss (see Wirtz 2007: 63). To reduce the amount of waste, Latitude Festival has colourful beer-cups fitting to the festival design that can be reused up to 100 washes. They offer as well return points with the possibility to donate the deposit for charity. The advantage is that people, who are too lazy to go back to the stall or do not mind losing two dollars if they throw away a cap, can do something for their good conscience, instead just throwing it away (see LF 2012).

An alternative option to treat the catering waste goes in line with the consistency approach (see p. 10). Subsequently, cups and plates are made of biological material, so done at the *Rothbury Festival* that only uses compostable serving materials (see RF 2011). Critical aspects are that they are difficult to recycle due to food remnants so that in comparison reusable cups have a much lower environmental impact (see. Dinkel 2010: 18). However, the correct waste separation is challenging as attendees need at first to know that the cups can be thrown in the compost bin. So RF simply uses the best place to communicate the message: right on the cups. There is written: "*One less plastic cup/ MADE OF CORN/ PEASE COMPOSTE IT*", (see Jones 2010: 316).

Though, some people do not read or care what the message on the cups is for. Therefore, RF uses manpower. Volunteers assisting the crowd to use the right bin, which are not stashed, rather highlighted with the same colours they got at the info sheet, downloadable on the website (see RF 2011). Of course waste volunteers are as well controller, who can observe the surrounding and the bin usage. T-shirts with the slogan *'One person who care'* worn by an easy-going team fitting to the festival crowd. They make it unlikely that attendees consciously use no or the wrong bin (see Jones 2010: 59).

Finally, despite the very best efforts, a festival will still cause much waste. The trash mountain, normally carefully hidden from the crowd, is the best communication argument to think about the daily profligacy. The *Splore Festival* has therefore installed the *trash palace*, where the whole load gets recycled. Of course it is far enough away from tents, stages and stalls, but still visible for everybody for somebody who walks along the festival site (see Splore 2012).

Water Management

A careful water management presumes a well-adapted water conservation strategy like deciding to take compost toilets, so done at the *Shambala Festival* (see SF 2012). If adequate sustainable solutions were found, there is still the question how to encourage the crowd to reduce water use. Probably the first thing coming into the mind are showers, providing water for thousands of festival attendees, as a key reason for water waste that needs to get managed. The *ECOCAMPING* association advises to install shower timer, time limiter or use coin-operated showers (see EC 2011).

If chosen water saving or water free toilets, a lot were achieved. However, a typical habit shown at festivals is the urinating in every corner, not in the provided toilets, probably as well because some of visitors like to save water. But this extreme amount of human urine is very harmful for the local ecosystems and its waterways. The basic thing to avoid that is to provide enough toilets and keep the toilets clean. Moreover, it is helpful to illuminate dark corners and control typical spots by a sustainability team. *Glastonbury Festival* set this under a campaign in corporation with Water Aid called *'Don't Take the* Piss' (see Jones 2010: 195 et seq.). Parallel to this they promoted the campaign *'love your loo'*, applying huge placards, info-spots, and even real toilets to promote the use as well as global water and sanitation issues. GF even does not miss the chance to draw attention to an eco-friendly toilet cleaner by communicating that the festival area is a farm and belongs to the cows, which want to get it back in a good condition. As well GF provides solvent-free hand sanitizer, which diminishes the use of water, important for hygiene issues and which is a nice service for the visitors – as well as the provision of eco-friendly shower crème, sponsored by a producer (see Jones 2010: 190 et seq.).

Figure 16: Polaroid of Billy Lunn & Charlotte Cooper, Members of the Band *The Subways* at Water Aid Backstage Bar at GF; Source: WaterAid 2011.

If there is a corporation with an NGO to provide water like *Vermont Brewers Festival* with *Food and Water Watch*, it is crucial for success to highlight the spot at the festival site.

If it is difficult to find, people get frustrated and could not get encouraged to avoid bottled water. When the festival provides tap-drinking water, every spot should be signed especially. It needs as well a visible verification that the water has been tested and is suitable for drinking as some visitors could have psychological barriers. Thirdly, information about the reasons for the tap-revival should be given, so done by *Peats Ridge Festival,* where is written on a placard that the festival is committed to reduce the amount of PET. This can also get realized by educational materials and volunteers of NGOs, specialised in waste and water management like *One difference* or *Hunter Water* (see Jones 2010: 318 et seq.).

6.4.3. Après-Festival Communication

If sustainability communication is well implemented during the festival, it should not be neglected afterwards. In the best case, festival attendees have understood that the organizers care about sustainability. Either way, they might go to the festivals homepage or the festivals' *facebook* page to look for some pictures or maybe they want to use the discussion forum for praises or complaints. Hence, the festival manger should watch the activities carefully. Reading the comments and response to open questions as well as to all mentioned sustainability issues, is very important to make the SC complete. It offers the opportunity to figure out further what was well done and what needs to be improved, explain some points attendees did not realized or give further information for those (became) really interested in the topic.

If sustainability has become an important issue for festival manager, it is convincing to publish the sustainability report, as *Falls Festival* has done. There interested stakeholder can have a look, which targets were set, achieved and what are the next steps.

Hence, it can help to present the festival as a responsible one (see for instance FF 2011b). It is interesting for visitors, but of course also for other stakeholders like the press, as it provides good material for their articles. Some fascinating, funny or emotional parts, which occur in the sustainability report, can be pointed out with a separate entry at the website and *facebook* page. For instance the honoring of the greenest stallholders or funny pictures made during NGO activities. These are things, which are able to touch people, remind people and get them to take action.

Figure 15 shows a good example from the NGO *WaterAid*. During their campaign at the GF they talked with artists at the backstage bar about their mission so that idols took pictures with a toilet for Water Aid. They have published this afterwards on their website, so that visitors suddenly recognize a broad support of famous people for their *'love your loo'*- campaign (see WaterAid 2011).

7. Empirical Study about the Expandability of Sustainability Communication through German Festivals

After examining what has already been done, the empirical part of this study investigates the important issues for implementing a sustainability communication strategy at German festivals and how this could be implemented. Therefore, research demand and design become clarified at the beginning before the evaluation presents the results of the survey.

7.1. Research Demand

In the area of sustainability communication through Open Air Music Festivals a high research demand can be attested. Firstly, SC, influenced by various scientific disciplines, is still new and does not yet have its specific theoretical framework (see Godemann/Michelsen 2011: 6). And apart from large businesses, most of the companies are inexperienced in SC. The typical situation for middle sized companies, although many already have implemented sustainable strategies, miss the chance to improve their images among the customers interested in sustainability (see Meiländer 2011: 52). Instead of green washing it is rather green hiding and it is annoying for the society that an opportunity to spread important sustainability solution is not taken.

The manager of music festivals are starting to care about the topic and wondering how strong they should communicate it. But many, if at all, have only some basic information presented on their website and are passive in this field, just adapting the necessary environmental standards.

Still others already worked out great initiatives which are a great opportunity to distribute ideas for a sustainable future, but do not present it appropriate for stakeholders, as recognizable at the *MS Dockville* festival (see p. 42). To achieve sustainability goals, it is especially important in this business to talk about it, because success very much depends on their attendees, for instance in emission and waste reduction. But Even if O'Neill (2009) found out that visitors awareness for sustainability issues has increased, it is hard to say, whether the same can be assumed for the German festival fans and moreover, it says nothing about the working SC strategy. Thus, there is insecurity around how much visitors do care for sustainability issues and above that how much they are willing to participate or how they can motivated to participate in improvement initiatives. It demands insights into costumers needs for creating a fitting communication strategy to achieve the best impact. But touching the customer is a tough task, as the fans of music festivals vary greatly. Hence, to figure this out, the analysis aims to answer the following questions:

- How much are visitors of music festivals interested in climate and environmental issues?
- Is the travel behaviour of festival goers more sustainable than others as they probably prefer festivals rather than air travels so that this can be integrated in SC?

- How much can the topic presented to the German attendees, subtle or slather?
- How do the German festival fans evaluate SC measures in particular, which were already adapted at other festivals?

With the results, festival operators are able to better estimate their customers and receive valuable information for the design of their SC strategy. For instance, it examines, whether it makes sense to focus on the ecological effect or rather the personal advantages by promoting a shuttle service. The results offer insights to improve SC in general and its role as a well working marketing instrument.

By knowing how to reach the customer, it further offers the chance to distribute SC among the festival operators and brings pressure to those, who have not yet cared about it. For this purpose, a cross-sectional analysis was conducted in the present survey to collect primary data for the research question (see Koschnick 1995: 532).

7.2. Research Design

As Schnell describes, the data mining and analysis is based on the research design, encompassing components like methods, selection process, instruments as well as derivation and justification of the posed questions (see Schnell et al 2011: 106). In general, the present inquiry is an explorative market research (see Altobelli 2007: 23). Acquisition method and survey instrument are described below.

Acquisition method and conduction of the survey

Several data acquisition methods exist. To investigate the present topic by applying the sampling strategy, an ad-hoc online-survey as method of quantitative research has been chosen. It is a quick and inexpensive way to collect a large amount of data and offers many technical advantages for controlling and data evaluation (see Thielsch 2008: 101). According to a study 72 per cent of the Germans and even 95 per cent in the 14 to 29 age group use the Internet (Bertsch et al 2011: 8). Hence, as festivals' target group has an especially high web affinity (see p. 21), an online survey can be seen as a fitting method. The method to distribute the survey among an online panel, as advised by Thielsch (see 2008: 97), was not used for the selection as this covers not exactly the targeted festival fans and would lead to scattering losses. Thus, it appears appropriate to ask festival operators to post a link to the survey on their *facebook* fanpage, as all of the named famous festivals have a fan page on this platform and *facebook* is the most used social network in Germany, used by 42 per cent of all web users and 72 per cent in the age of 14 to 29 (see Bertsch et al 2011: 5).

At first, on Monday, 06/02/2012, the festival operators of the most famous festivals, which have already showed willingness for greening the festival (see p. 29), were asked via E-Mail, including a link to the survey, to publish the survey at their *facebook* page. This ensured that the survey was widely distributed beyond the target group. Furthermore, it integrated automatically the *snowball system* as fans of the festival, which want to support the survey, activate the *'Like'* button or enter a comment. The corresponding information is then visible for their network. Scattering losses by this process are low as it is more likely that friends of festival fans are festival goers as well. Furthermore have people, who are not interested in festivals at all, much lower incentives to participate than those, registered in an online panel, where they get paid for participating in surveys. The operators of the *Haldern Pop* and the *Southside Festival* agreed to advertise the survey, published it on 07/02/2012 and 08/02/2012 and requested the results of the study in return. Due to the distribution, operators of the festival *Rocken am Brocken* became aware of the survey, asked via E-Mail for the results and spread the survey as well through their *facebook* fan page at the end of the week, on 10/02/2012. Thus, the survey has been published at three festival fan pages with the following key facts:

Table 2: Cooperating Festivals and Key Facts about them due to their Websites and Facebook Fanpages [07.03.2012].

Haldern Pop – A	Key facts
Location	Haldern
In operation Since	1981
Facebook Fanpage	.facebook.com/haldernpop
Visitors 2011 /Fans @facebook	7.000 /3.808
Genre	Folk, Indie, Indie Pop, Indie Rock, Britpop
Rocken am Brocken – B	**Key facts**
Location	Elend
In operation Since	1999
Facebook Fanpage	facebook.com/RockenAmBrocken
Visitors 2011/Fans @facebook	4000/5.492
Genre:	Rock, Indie, Alternative, Punk, Pop, Elektro
Southside Festival – C	**Key facts**
Location:	Neuhausen ob Eck
In operation since	2007
Facebook Fanpage	facebook.com/southsidefestival
Visitors 2011/Fans @facebook	50.000/54.661
Genre:	Indie, Rock, Pop

Figure 17: Festivals and their Location (A= Haldern Pop; B=Rocken am Brocken; C = Southside Festival

It is apparent that the operators of the long-established *Haldern Pop* have kept it small over all the decades, what keeps them at least among the ten most popular festivals in Germany (see p. 23) and brought them the *'European Festival Award'* for the best small festival (see EFA, 2012). Furthermore, a clear music trend is recognizable as the genres of all three festivals go in similar directions.

The *Rocken am Brocken* presents the newcomer, created by students from the *Hochschule Harz* just a few years ago (see Blanke/Hüttenrauch 2012). Extremely large, and the most famous festival, is the *Southside Festival* (see p. 23), so that their *facebook* page can reach a huge amount of potential survey participants. The distribution of the festivals illustrates that they cover different geographical areas so that it has been feasible to reach attendees from various German regions.

Survey Instrument: Questionnaire

The crucial survey instrument was a questionnaire, designed by the online panel website *http://www.q-set.de*, which fulfilled the requirements the author had regarding the software. Due to the wide dissemination it was necessary to ensure that a high amount of questions could get analysed for a reasonable price. Moreover, the software is very user-friendly and offers the creation of links to the survey, various possibilities for survey composition and different types of questions like matrix questions, multiple-choice and other options, which helped to create different response categories and to diversify the survey to make the responding process more interesting. It is also possible to create the survey in two languages, which was needed to reach foreign people like exchange students and tourists. Last but not least the site offers a pleasing design (see Q-Set 2012).

The survey design has been geared to be as short and concise as possible as the Internet is a restless place with many other interesting things to do (see Kuckartz et al. 2009: 34). This is more important, as the acquired people are not volunteers registered in an online panel to receive surveys. They are festival fans, which might be just curious, but not willing to spend much time on the survey.

Finally, the result has been a survey with 22 questions, distributed on two pages, to arrange it neatly and to reduce the frustration by the permanent need to click through the survey. In order to attract as well festival goers which are normally not environmentally conscious, it was entitled as *"Survey About The Sustainable Change Of Open Air Music Festivals"*. The imprecise meaning and broad utilization of the word sustainability helps to attract more people. Some might expect that it concerns general issues and then take part due to the *'year, whatever'*-heuristic. It means that humans sometimes do not pay enough attention to a topic and accept it, even if they would not decide for it consciously (see Thaler/Sunstein 2009: 38).

The questions were mainly designed half-open with several alternatives to capture different views, but to keep the comparability as well as to ensure a manageable evaluation. Questions, which imply that the responding person could like to add additional or other answers, were created as hybrid questions. This also provides deeper and interesting insights into the attendees view (see Schnell et al 2011: 311). Questions regarding sustainability communication at the event have a short explanation in front of the question as it is assumed that the most of the German festival fans have no experiences with those measures. That is also why the questions, which were more difficult to answer, were given the response possibility *'don't know'*.

Further, it has to be mentioned that the attendees were addressed with the informal *you*, to go in line with usual style of the festival operators in their external communication. In order to keep it short, the respond opportunity *'no answer'* was not given, but the questions were programmed in such a way that they did not need to get answered. After the questionnaire was created, several pre-tests (see Kuckartzet al. 2009: 37) were made with persons from the circle of acquaintances as well as with the *Q-Set* provider, which offer a questionnaire check as an additional service (see Q-Set 2012).

Regarding the terms of content the survey is divided into five main parts:

- Description of the sample (Socio-demographic characteristics; feelings about relevance of holidays comparing to festivals, important general aspects of festival participation);

- Holiday and festival travel behaviour (Q. 1-6, ask especially for importance of holiday trips and aircraft usage);

- Environmental measures (Q. 7-9, ask for its importance comparing to other festival aspects, role in the framework program and its general importance for attendees);

- Explicit Sustainability Measures (Q. 10-18, ask for opinion about implementation of concrete sustainability measures in the areas of mobility, catering, procurement, waste and sustainable lifestyle);

- Remarks (question without numbering, gives the opportunity to add comments).

Due to appropriate precision explained above, it was not possible to ask for all the measures or go into more details. Hence, those measures were focused, which were especially dependent on visitor contribution. Things like installing timers for showers to encourage water saving does not need an offensive communication in advance.

The answers to the questions and the additional remarks of the attendees offer interesting insights and allow inferences to other sustainability issues. At the end of the survey the E-Mail address is provided, in case somebody should be interested in results or has specific questions, which should be answered. Indeed, this has been used several times.

7.3.   Evaluation of the Survey

The following pages publish the results of the survey, which can be viewed in appendix 5. To make it easier to follow and to stay in line with working areas for sustainability management (see p. 27), the classification of the findings has been structured conveniently. But in front of the single categories, the return and opinions regarding sustainability measures become presented in general.

7.3.1. Return

Distributing a survey in a social network makes it difficult to analyse a return rate. However, shortly after the survey has been published by the Southside-fan-page, the server of *Q-Set* crashed and was not available for three hours, what might have led to return losses. In total was the link to the survey spread by 63 clicks on the *'Like'*-button (see appendix 4). This leads to a further distribution. As the survey has been closed on 16/02/2012, the following results were achieved:

Table 3: Respond to the Questionnaire; Source: Author.

Festival Fans who...	Number	Percentage
...replied to the questionnaire	751	48,6%
...accessed the questionnaire without response	793	51,4%
Sum	1544	100,0%

Hence, nearly 50 % of the people following the link have answered the questions. Furthermore, it came out that once they started answering the questions, only 16,8 % have provided an incomplete questionnaire, what implies that scope and form of the survey were deemed to be appropriate (see Jakob et al 2009: 123 et seq.). Beside this, it can be said that the want to contribute with own insights was high. Participants have given many additional comments regarding their own feelings, additional ideas for improvement or own evaluations of already experienced measures, what indicates a high interest in this topic (see appendix 6 et seq.).

7.3.2. Description of the Festival Fan Sample

Form the first part of the survey, the following socio demographic profile of the sample emerged. Firstly can be recognized that music festivals seems to have only a small amount of tourists as the English questionnaire was only answered by 1,1 % of the total number of participants, what correlates to at least 8 persons responding to the questions. Furthermore, no significant difference in gender participation exists as the women's share is with 50,9 % barely higher than the proportion of men with 49,1 %. Regarding to the age distribution of the participants the findings appearing mostly consistent with the ascertained age structure (see p. 24). However, as assumed there is a larger gap between the early and the late twenties. Due to the changing circumstances, an additional division between 18 and 29 was given.

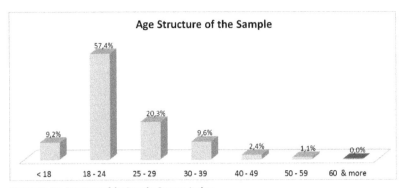

Figure 18: Age Structure of the Sample; Source: Author.

In this respect, it is confirmed that the festivals are especially interesting for people in the typical age for education and vocational training. Nevertheless, adding the participants between the ages of 25 and 39, one third of the participants are young employees. These specifications conform to the information about occupation, which present that more than 40 % are university students, nearly one third are school students or apprentice and a quarter is employed. The high amount of students is likely due to the proven fact that the higher the individual is educated and informed, the more he or she is interested in sustainability issues (see p. 14). It becomes more obvious that the target group was reached, because only 3 % answered 'none' to the question, which festivals they have already visited. This also includes people, who went to a festival for the first time in 2012, which is recognizable by personal comments and by the differences between the Q. 1 and Q. 2. Nearly 10 % answered that they have not visited a festival in 2011, but only 1,3 % said the same regarding their plans for 2012.

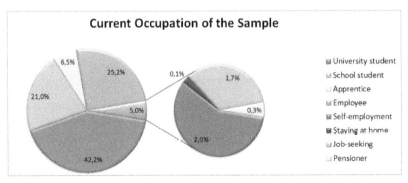

Figure 19: Current Occupation of Participants; Source: Author.

Most of the festival fans visited one festival in 2011, but apparently also the most of the participants plan to add one or two events in 2012, as the share of two visits increased by 12 % and the share of three times by 3 %. More than three festivals seem to be less attractive for the attendees as those

75

numbers dropped down. This emphasizes that festivals are special events, an expensive pleasure for the typical fan - well reflected in many additional comments. It evokes the *'once in a year'*-attitude, whereby they allow themselves misbehaviour regarding every conceivable life situations that they normally control (see Thaler/Sunstein 2009: 43 et seq.).

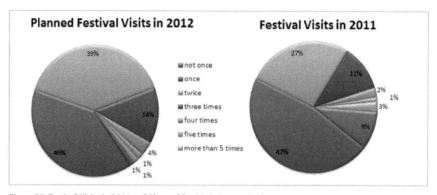

Figure 20: Festival Visits in 2011 and Planned for 2012; Source: Author.

It is interesting to look at which typical aspects are most important for a festival participation. Thereto still research demand exists as they offer remarkable insights into the motivations for a festival visit (see p. 24). The research found out that *'meeting new people'* is not that important for the most of the particpants, whereto only 14 placing a high value on. Fitting to that it is striking that *'spending much time with friends'* is very important for nearly 70 % of those questioned. It is even more important than the stated *'Line Up'*, meaning the list of the artists, which 67 % consider as very important. This illustrates clearly that for the individuals the community is paramount, what offers great hints for creating the sustainabity communication concept. Also the typical *'sleeping in a tent'* is not that meaningful to the participants as the distribution among advocates and opponents is nearly 50-50. Reading the additional survey comments it is reasonable to suppose that this is due to the often mentioned mess at the camp site, in relation to waste and the as anarchy described behaviour of some attendees, so that people feel uncomfortable (see comments to appendix 6).

Thus, it is not surprising that the most significant issue for the sample is a *'relaxed atmosphere'*. This broad consensus could of course suggest that this is to be expected, but comparing the answers with the comments it is obvious that many participants have had negative experiences and feel annoyed by visitors believing that misbehaving beongs to the festival feeling. This is emphazised by ofen made additional statements in terms of safetey which was thematised nine times in the comment box. Hence, they want enough security, first aid paramedic as well as police, even if these things are sometimes bugging (see appendix 6).

Regarding the sanitary installations nearly the half agreed that this is very imporant and 40 % that it is imporant for them. Hence, even if it is hard to realize everytime, clean facilities are not surprisingly significant elements contributing to the sense of well-being and prevent contamination of the area. The great approval for free parking confirms the high share of car users as well as the challenge to reduce private transport.

Cheap food is for the most of the sample less significant. Many people mostly eat the food they have brought and others do not really expect cheap food and accept higher prices (as the visit happens just once or twice a year anyway). More details on this issue in 7.3.7.

The question includes as well the aspect *Envrionmental protection measures of operators*. As it is only one of several points, it will rather be answered honestly without or with less thinking about social desirability (see Mummendey 1995: 223 et seq.). However, for at least 48 % it is important and nearly 20 % even find it very important so that the numbers together show that considerably more than two thirds pay attention to it. Hence, managers have to be prepared that fans do look for their sustainability efforts.

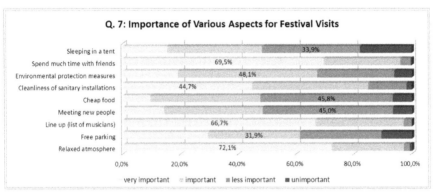

Figure 21: Q. 7 - Importance of Various Aspects for Festival Visits; Source: Author.

7.3.3. Sustainability Measures in General

Afterwards, the sample has been asked what they think about stronger engagement in environmental and climate protection measures of festival operators. The notion *sustainability* was not stated to avoid confusions and misinterpretations. The pro-environmental attitude, already apparent in other studies (see BMU 2010), gets confirmed as well. Only 11,5 % does not think that those measures are very important or important. Hence, 43 % say it is very important and 45 % indicate it is an important issue. Comparing to the still high, but apparently lower approval in the question above, it shows that many participants answered honestly as so far climate and environmental protection measures of operators do not affect their decision, whether they go to a festival or not. But nevertheless, this does not change the fact, that they would appreciate more ambitions.

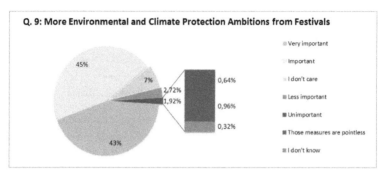

Figure 22: Q. 9: Opinions About General Environmental & Climate Protection Measures of Festival Managers; Source: Author.

The survey participants emphasize this impression with related remarks in the comment box at the end of the questionnaire. Thus, comments regarding the general contribution of festivals contains for instance that it is a great and important topic, that there is a lot to do and that fun and sustainability would not be mutually exclusive. One person said perfectly summarizing: *"Festival are huge events. I go there due to the great bands. Everything what has to do with Environmentalism at festival, do I support!"*, (see 'Generally', appendix 7)

One person adds that bands should be integrated: *"Why not involve the artists and musicians in the sustainable festival concept. Many of them already have an interest in this and they could help to make a "hot" topic out of it"*, (see 'Bands', appendix 7). This topic was not treated in the questionnaire as the function of role models is quite clear, should and is used by festival as already presented in 6.4.

But despite these results and the high contribution, many people do really doubt that others are interested in those measures. They rather belive that the most attendees only think about party and alcohol and not about environmentalism at all. Some commentators present this point of view that they do not want to overtake responsibility and that this would only be the case of operators, what is indeed only a marginal share of the whole sample (see 'No Interest', appendix 7).

The disparities between the own and the supposed opinion clarifies that there exist, despite the presence in the media, a great lack in public recognition, perception and discussion about personal and businesses abilities to influence a sustainable development. It makes also obvious that the majority of people despite their opinion and despite the results Leitzmann et al got (see p. 66), still believe that environmentalism has a low coolness factor as they do not acknowledge publically to it. This is almost the complete opposite comparing to other things like specific brands. Hence, thinking about this makes clear that the audience in comparison to the early festivals has changed vital. The guiding principle of the first festival generation was to create a better world, treating with love, peace, freedom as well as environmentalism resulting in a common feeling to be different than the rest of the society and rebellious. Now, participants also want to be special, free and feel rebellious, but, probably - due to the point that nobody really feels threatened by sustainability issues (see p. 16) - with a different interpretation. This perception underlines further the major challenge to design the communication concept target-group-adequate, as already presented in chapter 6.4. Beyond that it displays the necessary sensitivity to reach the desired change in behaviour. What this means for specific situations, becomes obvious in the following parts.

7.3.4. Tickets and Mobility

The question of the distance from home to the festival reveals that most of the festival attendees pay close attention to the approach route. Indeed is nearly a quarter of the visited festivals, where the route does not exceed 50 km. Almost half of the visitors are up to 250 km away, corresponding to a journey from Magdeburg to Bremen. Hence, festivals are a rather regional events and the numbers encourage that fans can be animiated through an attractive offer and the fitting communication to make greater use of public transport. So the longer the distances the less attractive it gets, depending on additional wating periods, more train changes and higher prices.

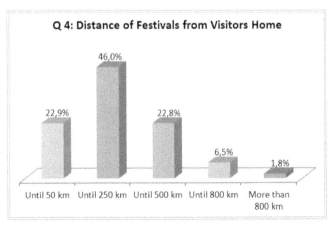

Figure 23: Q. 4: Distance of Festivals from Attendees Home; Source: Author.

Regarding the personal transport needs the investigation notably shows that the festival fan does not travel in more environmental friendly way than other tourists. More than a half uses the car for their holiday trips, followed by plane use and after that public transport (comparing to Ifak Institut 2009), whereby 30 % stated that they use once in a year the plane for their holidays. Nearly 10 % use it for several private trips yet. But also 16 % agreed that they would likely go on an additional flight without the festival dates what avoids additional carbon emissions. That means, festivals contribute seemingly to the reduction of greenhouse gases, but it is by far not convincing enough to sell it as a great climate protection contribution to the stakeholders.

What can apparently be sold to festival goers, and therewith additionally as a sustainability measure for stakeholders, are carbon offset tickets. Indeed suprisingly 53 % see it as a good idea to contribute. For further 15 % it is at least a possiblity to silence their conscience and 16 % find that they have not enough income at the moment to spend additional money for those measures. Even if the income level is not obvious, it shows nevertheless that they generally appreciate this measures.

Thus, in sum 82 % are in favour of those tickets and 68 % stated they would buy it. Moreover 44 persons of the sample added comments to this question. Some points were remarkable. Many find it better to integrate an additional fee for those purposes in the ticket price. Some say it, because it is easier to handle, others as they think it is a good idea, but do not believe that they would decide for it on a volunatry base. The third group means that ticket prices are often so high that this already should empossible these charges (see appendix 8). This is in line with psychological science describing it as the *'year, whatever'*-heuristic, which has also been mentioned earlier (see Thaler/Sunstein 2009: 38). Beside that, opponents argue either that they pay enough, that they are pro cliamte warming or that they simply find it ridiculous. Another person reflected that there is no guarantee for the right usage of the additional spended money. Proponents mentioned as well the need for transparency, that they want to support a reasonable project and want to know, whether the money reaches the project (see appendix 8), what further underlines the demand for a comprehensive communication strategy.

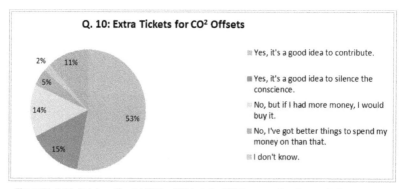

Figure 24: Q. 10: Opinions About Additional Tickets for CO2-Compensation; Source: Author.

This should definitely include background information about the effectiveness of measuers as some comments showed that people refuse participation due to missing or wrong information. For instance one person said he or she would not buy it as reforestation was not a climate protection measure, because if biomass rots it releases combined carbon dioxide. There would be more reasonable approaches. This totally underrated the long term and signifiant role of forests for CO_2-saving, which is better than technical solutions demanding additional input of energy.

Some attendees, which are against it, substantiate this position with alternatives they would prefer. They rather like to support efficiency measures to reduce energy consumption, to exchange classical lighting or generally enhance the waste deposit. Others argue in favor of more measures right linked to the festival like barbecue areas, bus shuttles as well as the common prohibition of brought camping furniture (laying around afterwards), (see appendix 8).

As mentioned it was not possible to integrate any possible measure in the questionnaire, but due to the great carbon reduction possiblities, attendees were asked for amenities convincing them to use a shuttle service. It stands out that, even if most of them arrive by car, only 17 % marked none of the arguments would be convincing and they rather take the car.

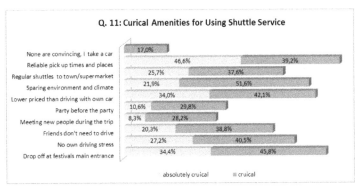

Figure 25: Q. 11: Share of the Sample who said that the Presented Amenities are Crucial or Very Crucial; Source: Author.

The others could imagine to use the service, if it fulfills some aspects. It is absoluteley crucial for nearly 90 % that pick up times and places are reliable. Somebody commented that they already used a festival shuttle service, but due to delay they had to catch a taxi to finally arrive at home, what was more expensive and destroyed the carbon saving effect. This argument is followed closely by 'Drop off at festivals main entrance', which is for 80 % a convincing argument. Understandably, because the especially long waiting hours in front of the entrance to the peak time loads is nerve-wracking for visitors. But without saving money or at least a good offer, they rather would not decide for the shuttle service. A reasonable price is the third most imporant argument. People, who have left a comment, often intend to provide combined tickets including discounts. However, it is also recognizable that for 52 % 'Sparing climate and environment' is crucial and for one-fifth it is indeed absoluteley crucial, what shows that nearly three quarters think about their environmental impact and show willingness to reduce it. Further arguments, which should be used to promote the service are 'Avoiding own driving stres's and the information that the festival offers reuglar shuttle services, as without having the possibility to even shop for missing things made many shy away.

Only a miniority is interested in celebrating in front of the festival. Also meeting new people is only for one third an interesting aspect, which fits to the already predictable result that festival fans mostly want to spend time with their friends. As anticipated, participants often additionally mentioned that the baggage prevents them from using the shuttle service (see 'Travel', appendix 7). It further highlights the need for a comprehensive approach, meaning that providing a shuttle service means as well to consider supporting services like the mentioned supermarket or a tent rental service to reduce heavy or cumbersome baggage.

7.3.5. Framework Program

Providing a framework program at the festival is a tough task as musicians are the main acts and it is difficult to estimate, which action could destroy the atmosphere. Indeed, in answering the question, which items presented on the framework program in the diagram would be interesting, said on average 32 % for each one that it is not interesting, 18 % that is rather not interesting and 16 % on average being indecisive.

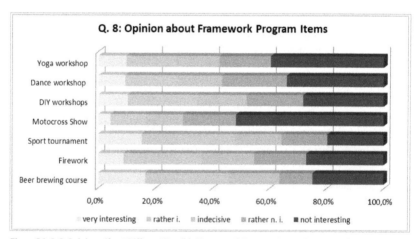

Figure 26: Q. 8: Opinions About Different Possible Framework Program Items; Source: Author.

Thus, it was not surprising that one third of the commentators does refuse additional activities as they find it unimportant and want to focus on the music. Comparing to that were two thirds of the comments devoted to additional suggestions of what else can be done. They add ideas especially containing the contribution of visitors and learning effects, like barbecue workshops or barbecue competitions. Others are especially interested in DIY, pick up the example of furniture building as well as shelter building or to do handicrafts in general. They add activities in the theme of creating fashion and accessories. Many suggest theatre or music workshops, which seem indeed natural to a music event. Even discussion rounds about societal topics, one person said together with musicians, were suggested (see appendix 9).

Obviously many customers are definitely interested in spending their time with doing something new or special during the festival weekend. Beside those integrative parts, there were given the non-sustainable answering options *'Firework'* and *'Moto cross show'* to assess the samples attitude towards it. Remarkably, the motocross-show, which is of course not often integrated in festivals and a conspicuous intervention, reaches the lowest acceptance. A firework with its romantic character, and as a typical ending of an event, is much more popular and earns an approval of 36 %. The most popular sport tournament is for nearly 50 % very or rather interesting. Sporting free time activities have several advantages like being of course environmental friendly, enabling movement, fun as well as a challenge and involve many people from participants to audience. Beside that it does not need as much space, attention and money comparing to a motocross-show.

The same naturally applies even more to the announced workshops. They thrive on small groups coming together so that they barely disturb non-interested festival fans, but offer instead some curious people to test it themselves. Interestingly receives the DIY offers approval from one third (35 % very interested and rather interested), which is more than typical trend activities like dancing or yoga achieve.

It shows that among the young generation definitely exists a demand to enable themselves in doing or creating things on their own, what has become neglected in the modern society and which is a meaningful instrument for sustainable development (see p. 11). Therewith, operators have the opportunity to contribute in sustainable development and adding inexpensive but interesting aspects to the festival.

Presenting framework items, which are specifically referring to a sustainable lifestyle, the research found out that the samples' interest is remarkably higher than for the other examples. Specifically they were asked:

"At Glastonbury Festival is one area dedicated to specific ways for a sustainable lifestyle. With the help of NGOs visitors can test how to charge batteries with a bicycle, contribute to discussions, learn how to get started urban gardening and listen to the bands performing there. What's your opinion on this?", (see Q. 14).

It replied that more than 50 % said that it would be an interesting offer for them. Nearly 42 % said that they do not want to care about those issues during the festival.

The given additional comments, presented in the diagram by *'Alternative answers'*, can be broken down into three main parts. Many added, even if they cannot imagine how it fits to the festival that they normally like to address those matters. Others are simply indecisive how to judge it and the last group says, it is *"cool"*, *"a good offer"* and it would depends mainly on the current line-up, whether they would attend it or not. Only 1,1 % is not interested in caring about it at all, what is an astonishing small amount illustrating again the strong interest in sustainability issues among the society and as well in the younger generation - even if nearly nobody believes it (see appendix 9).

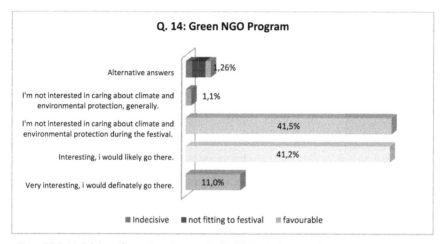

Figure 27: Q. 14: Opinions About a Green Program Realized by NGOs; Source: Author

7.3.6. Sale of Goods

This part consists of the opinions about the food and non-food sector as well as sustainably acting sponsoring partners.

Regarding the latter, the sample was asked, whether festival sponsors should fulfil sustainability criteria. Almost the half (49 %) thinks that businesses should be selected, which take a persuasive stand for climate and environment protection. But still many participants say this is exaggerated (17 %) and even 25 % do not care. Comparing to other questions arise a high amount, namely 9 %, who selected the answering possibility *"I don't know"*.

Associating to the higher environmentalism they have shown in previous questions, it publishes the understandable common lack in knowledge regarding business opportunities, as it is difficult to estimate what businesses should do, are able to do and what are alternatives. Some might be frightened that focusing sustainable acting companies means representatives with a typical eco image not fitting to the festival, what would underline that the dusty eco image is still in the heads of the participants or has at least a negative connotation.

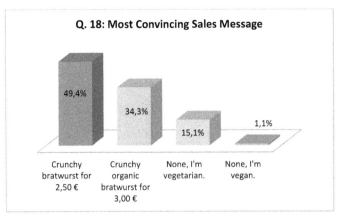

The indications getting stronger by looking at the question, whether they would decide for a '*Bio-Bratwurst*', which costs 50 cent more in the given scenario, or take a normal one for 2,50 €. Almost 50 % decided for the normal bratwurst and only a third for the organic one. Interestingly, announce 15 % that they are Vegetarian, what is more than twice the amount than the national average is (7,3 %, see Pape et al 2012: 6). 1,1 % point out that they eat *only* vegan food so that there is at least a demand for it. This is pleasant in sustainability terms, but induces as well that nearly 60 % of the meat eating attendees would take the conventional bratwurst, even the majority quoted at the beginning that cheap prices are less important. This was promising that even organic and regional food, which could be more expensive, is saleable.

Apart from the topic, it makes obvious tha the participants do care less for things like social desirability and that the given answers are honestly (see p. 58).

However, it cannot be assumed that this share is not interested in welfare of animals or do not care for foods' quality. The problem lies elsewhere. It shows the doubtful recognition of *bio* or *organic* within the society. On the one hand has bio has been tarnished by various scandals inducing decreasing trust in the products. Simultaneously, people feel confronted with an annoying bio-labelling everywhere appealing too intrusive and evokes denials.

This goes in line with the comments some of the sample left. One person indeed demands the provision of more vegan food. But several people remark that bio is not always better than conventional food and that there exists a high risk of abuse. They claim especially that foods from foreign countries, travelling thousands of kilometres, are labelled as organic and that too many labels with different criteria subsist. Another point of criticism concerns the prices at the festival. The sample demands a pricing, which can be considered to be fair, avoids the wasteful purchase of canned food and is therewith able to reduce baggage (see 'Food', appendix 7).

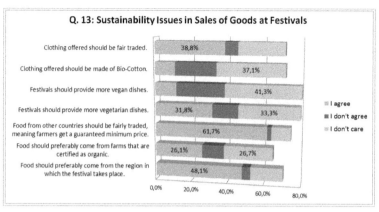

Figure 29: Q. 13 Sustainability Issues in Sales of Goods; Without Answering Possibilities 'I don't know' and 'It's not that Important to me'; Source: Author.

Hence, festivals should deliberate to dispose moderate food prices, for instance by providing the mentioned festival supermarket, so that less baggage is needed and enourage visitors to use public transport. Furtheremore, could a large share of the food stall demand be covered by regional providers, when less stalls are needed. Regional supply is an important point for many survey participants, also recognizable due to the results of Q. 13. There, almost the half of the respondents disagreeded and only 26 % agreed that food should come from organic farms.

Remarkably is as well that two third think the food should be fair traded, against what only 2,2 % do not agree. Here, a great difference can be faced. While *bio* is struggling with distrust and incomprehensibility, a difficulty like price dumping in poorer countries is obviously a comprehensible problem with a clearly offered solution and which has already been braodly communicated so that it earns a broad aggreement.

This is probably an unexpected result among party people. Even for clothes, where the sample barely cares for bio cotton (11,3 %), fair trade is for almost 40 % an imporant issue. Supplementary it is interesting that, despite the refusing stance by organic food, wish rather 32 % of the sample more vegetarian dishes, even if only 15 % said earlier that they are vegetarians. It demonstrates that the sample is interested in vegetarian food no matter because they want to reduce their meat consumption, want to take responsibility for climate or just like to eat more vegetables. It demonstrates as well that meatless meals have reached a broad acceptance among young adults.

Apart from that, bio has obviously an image problem and it needs meaningful statements for the broad audience communication emphasizing transparency and good living conditions. Nevertheless, it is important to deliver organic food as more and more people beyond the audience and other stakeholders care for it as important issue for SD.

7.3.7. Waste

The last point obtains very much attention. Already in Q. 7, where the sample was asked for important festival aspects, they claimed in addition a clean festival site. Referring to Q. 10, some suggested instead of CO_2-compensating measures to rather increase waste deposits or to prohibit additional camping gear, allow only reusable cup and to improve waste separation. Many mention at several points that they really dislike the *'I don't care'*-mentality. There was furthermore a great contribution in adding suggestions to reduce the waste problem. So, one person likes the initiative by the *Summer Breeze Festival*, where posters for three submitted bin bags are given away. In the same direction goes the hint that it should be possible to hand in deposit bottles and other items which are not needed anymore to reduce the baggage. Easier to realize should be suggestions like the extension of return times for reusable beakers or the provision of more and different bin bags enabling the attendees to improve their waste separation (see 'waste', appendix 7).

The results of the waste related questions reflect likewise a keen awareness. There, 90 % would bring own bottles and dishes which can be used when food gets bought and wherewith they get water for free, so for instance done at the *LiB*. Only 3 % consider it as exaggerated. One notes that this could probably be uncomfortable, what might be true (see appendix 10). Even if the most carrying around a drink, they would not walk around with a plate as well or walking every time back to the campsite. Hence, those dishes could be mainly used at the campsite. Another comment to avoid plastic waste encourages the provision of cutler at the beginning. This should be bought again if it gets lost (see appendix 10). Moreover, encouraging the crowd to take this along, means consequently to provide appropriate options, as they were already mentioned, to leave other items or food at home.

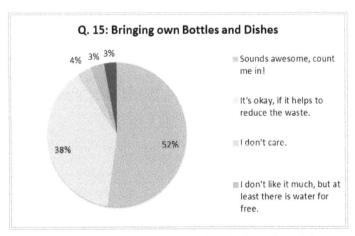

Figure 30: Q. 15: Opinions about Bringing Own Bottles and Dishes to the Festival; Source: Author.

Similar reactions arose as it was described that the *Isle of Wight Festival* informs that it needs 485 hours to remove camping gear, costing a lot of money, which could be better used for entertainment. The feedback showed that the sample faces the same situation at German festivals and they really dislike this attitude. Thus, 62 % are really astonished that so many leave their tents at the campsite and 24 % rather agree on that. In sum 71 % totally or rather agree that it makes them angry and even 61 % think that they will pay more attention once they were confronted with those numbers. Comparing to that only 12 % say that they have not thought about this yet, against what almost 40 % totally disagree. So this is apparently a serious problem for festival goers, which negatively effects their well-being and the atmosphere.

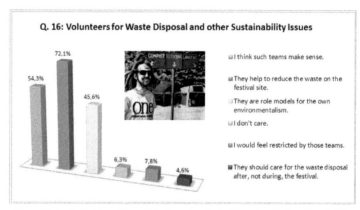

Figure 31: Q. 16: Opinions About Volunteers for Waste Disposal and other Sustainability Issues; Source: Author, Picture: Overbeck, L. (2012).

Q. 16 was related to volunteers who work at *Rothbury Festival*, where a team works under the headline *'One person who cares'* for waste avoidance and a correct separation. Thereto, a picture was shown to give the sample an idea how this could look like and to avoid false notions. The answers proove that the postive attribute outweighs significantly. Only 8 % indicate that they would feel restricted. Even less find waste management is something that should be treated afterwards. The samples' comments go in different directions. Some add especially that they are able to separate waste on their own as they do this all the time and do not need help. Others claim it could be annoying or they could feel controlled.

The other way around some are concerned that many attendees will annoy volunteers with inappropriate comments. One assumes the risk that visitors think they do not need to tidy, because the volunteers will do it. Another person does not believe that waste really gets seperated and sees only additional emissions by appointing volunteers. But various would appreciate such *"slight pressures"*, say this makes sense and would be sometimes even essential, especially on the campsite. Apart from the demand, many say it depends especially on volunteers' behaviour as they should conduct themselves with charm and humour and not stress the crowd or play strict teachers to them.

So, volunteers could be helpful. With a view on other demands, like safety, left tents or first aid issues, they could support progress in various fields. Though, the results underline the need for a sensitive collection and training of those volunteers as otherwise positive effects could be destroyed and even influence the festivals' athmosphere. But a well selected team of festival fans, which gets probably through volunteering the chance to participate and which becomes recognition (in terms of appropriate incentives like free time during the festival, tickets for the next year, etc.) will certainly be motivated to support it suitably.

Apart from that it is a good example demonstrating again the needed sensitivity and the correct design of all communication channels to succeed. A feeling of how this could look like provides the following concept for sustainability communication, which is based on the insights of this analysis.

8. Derived Sustainability Communication Concept

After treating many interesting but maybe overwhelming insights, it makes sense to formulate a communication concept giving orientation and comprising the measures and instruments for an adequate, creative and feasible SC concept. To become familiar with the development of a communication concept, the first part introduces briefly types and functions, which get applied here, while the second part concerns the demands for treating SC as concept topic plus the procedure of developing the concept.

8.1. Types and Functions of Communication Concepts

Schmidbauer and Knödler-Bunte, experts for marketing communication, see the communication concept as the *"heart of communication planning"* (2004: 14), as the *"most important navigation instrument"* (2004: 14) and as *"hinge between communication problem and communication solution"* (2004: 13). Apparently, it is a very important instrument to match the communication challenges, but often not sufficiently exploited so that potentials to get the communication on a comprehensible and convincing track remained unused. Less visually they say it is a methodically developed and clearly structured planning instrument, which is used as practical guide, a planning guide for economic decisions, as well as to motivate participants, minimize risks and to support and prepare strategic decision making (2004: 10 et seq.). Nonetheless, the communication measures can only help to strengthen existing needs or opinions or change the direction moderately and to use this for the communication target, but it is not possible to change the target group itself (see 2004: 20).

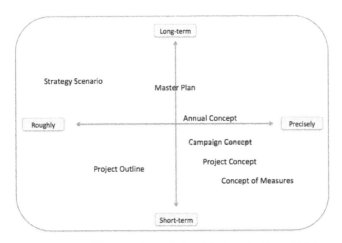

Figure 32: Types of Concepts, Source: Author, following Schmidbauer/Knödler-Bunte, 2004:24.

Schmidbauer and Knödler-Bunte moreover provide an overview about the different communication concept types, for instance strategy scenario, annual concept and others, whose time horizon and level of detail is demonstrated above.

The demand for a strategic orientation in SC is pretty much the same as for other products or services in the communications policy. Weis recommends the following scheme, which makes it noticeable that the strategic orientation is the initial point for the deduction of targets and operative measures (see Weis 2007: 181):

Figure 33: Communication Concept Scheme; Source: Author, based on Weis 2007: 182.

The following concept can be classified as a master plan, as it provides much more concrete issues as a strategic scenario and includes concrete measures comprising all fields of communication, summarizes in addition and is based on a previous analysis and strategic guidelines. Moreover, it outlined some aspects in more detail. Not included are parts of the detail planning like working and budget planning and the schedule. Due to that it presents the specific action demands and guidance (see Schmidbauer/Knödler-Bunte 2004: 24).

To create a convincing communication concept the following characteristics should be included (see Schmidbauer/Knödler-Bunte 2004:16 et seq.).

- Simplicity of presentation to avoid lack of understanding due to technical terms or complicated extensive descriptions, regarding efforts, should not be visible

- Careful analysis; including situation check, analysis and comprehensiveness

- Derived replicable conception strategy considering all concept appropriate, but not all possible, variables as there is the risk to lose focus what often leads to a reduced controllability

- Intelligent and creative solutions, which are able to set it apart from the standard ones, but nevertheless by delivering...

- Realistic and pragmatic solutions so that creative solutions stay in sensible proportion to personnel, capacity and economic conditions

For the following master plan, the communication policy scheme of Weis can be adapted, but in a more detailed form. For sustainability communication, the target is to raise sustainability compatible behaviour of the stakeholder. The determination and realization of the communication policy depends then on the specific conditions of where and when the measures should be placed.

Equipped with knowledge about communication concept deployment, the next part shows how a SC concept can be designed for the research topic.

8.2. Sustainability Communication Concept for Open Air Music Festivals

Once the strategy development leads to an integration of sustainability management and an appertaining SC, it is just the question how to proceed. This demands a comprehensive analysis of the market, the own business and its SC strategy, competitors and customers (see Weis 2007: 45 et seq.). The communication concept presents the main aspects, which are essential for the derived communication strategy. The business analysis is logically not feasible in a general concept. However, hints regarding aspects, which should be considered are given subsequent.

Based on the analyses the challenges for communication can be examined and adequate communication targets can be set. Afterwards concrete recommendable measures with notes for realization and some convincing KPIs are presented derived from successful implemented initiatives by sustainable oriented festivals and from the results of the costumer survey.

8.2.1. Analysis

The analyses, according to a marketing management process, comprehends the situation in the own business, the market conditions and the customer with their demands and relevant competitors (see Weis 2007: 45 et seq.).

Market Analysis

The matter being researched here, normally by using qualitative and quantitative market data (see Weis 2007: 49), obtains the question, whether the market is susceptible to sustainable measures. Indeed, has sustainability some specialties comparing to considerations for products.

Consequently, there is or at least should be a high demand to sustainability measures in the market. Firstly, from the businesses point of view, because they do not want to spend much money on delayed adjustment policies due to institutional regulations. This could be for instance the extension of carbon trade or a rising oil price so that it gets very expensive, if traders are no locals. Secondly, from the customers' view as most of them care for sustainability measures and would of course also appreciate if those lead to cost savings so that the price can be kept constant. And thirdly, from the societal position the *'commodity'* sustainability is undoubtedly irreplaceable what has to lead to high reputation effect in the future, if it is trustfully and well managed.

Despite that, according to sustainability matters at music festivals exists still a low 'market saturation' with very much potential regarding sustainability initiatives, but as well with more and more changing actors in the scene introducing probably a change in festival management.

Competitor Analysis

In this general conception this point gives of course no specific hints. A broad analysis of the state of the art initiatives are given in 7.3 (see p. 54 et seq.), presenting the great efforts of some festivals really integrating sustainable measures and SC in their management. Nevertheless, some do not present themselves as good as they could - probably due to the mentioned concerns that it could look too green. The rising number of public activities as well as the increasing contribution to greening-competitions (e. g. AGFA), show that a sustainable trend is visible, no matter whether it happens because of costumer demands, recognition of adaption needs or due to an increasing intrinsic motivation.

Festival manager should view important competitors, which offer the same artists, are close to the own location or provide a similar atmosphere. If those festivals publish sustainability effectively, ambivalent festival fans probably prefer the responsible looking one, as the majority cares for sustainability issues (see p. 54 et seq.).

Business Analysis

Before thinking about sustainability, the festival operators must be clear about the fesival's typcial background, values, philosophy, history, the specific characterisitcs of their cutomers (see p. 19) and of course about the available capital, what normally is the bottleneck for communiacation plans (see Schmidbauer/ Knödler-Bunte 2004: 36 et seq.). The difference is here that shifting the methods can help to reduce costs pluse increase the image in the long run. Not to forget to think about those artists already support climate and environmental protection and typical guests at the own festival. They can be included and will likely love to support respective initiatives.

If these points were examined it can be considered, how the businesses SC strategy must look like to fit in the festival design, including things like the presentation of the message – subtle or slather (see p. 32). As typical for changing processes, a businesss should therefore carry out a current-state-analysis in order to deduce proper measures, where the message is recognizable and the festivals strengths get used for communication (see Wöhe 2005: 97 et seq.).

Customer Analysis

The typical festival visitor is... - this sentence is generally hard to complete. Music fans are a heterogeneous group. Though, some characteristics are conspicuous due to the results of the conducted survey (see p. 55 et seq.):

- **Socio- demographic attributes:**
  - About the same number of males or females
  - The age between 18 and 24 is dominating → mainly school or university students and young employees

- **Psychographic attributes:**
  - Friends have a high priority
  - Festival are seen as special events, where they want to feel free and set aside everything else
  - Addicted to specific band/musicians, which are crucial for the festival visit
  - Mainly believe climate and environmental protection is important, but ...
    - One part still perceives it as an unattractive topic and does not want to look or to be too eco-like (could reduce recognition in pear group)
    - The others stand openly and publicly by their opinion so that they are very interested in related information and program points

Thus, those characteristics influence SC strategy remarkably and need to be considered for the concept development.

8.2.2. Communication Challenge and Targets

Facing the results of the analyses it is becoming clear that the image is the biggest problem of sustainability measure, because:

- The traditional picture of scruffy environmentalists
- Some measures are seen as dictatorial imposed and limiting ('environmental dictatorship')
- Opaqueness of information and missing reliability

Therefore, the target for SC is to design it for the target group in a sympathetic and comprehensible manner, achieving attention and meeting the claims on reliability, effectiveness regarding the sustainable targets as well as attractiveness. Thus, it appeals not in the eyes of uninterested attendees in the frumpy eco style, but they rather feel attracted by the initiatives and particular behaviours become a naturally part of the festival participation and probably beyond.

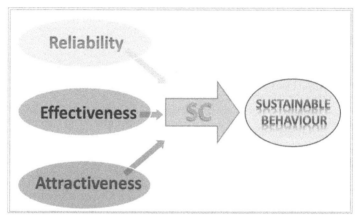

Figure 34: Crucial Aspects for a Convincing Sustainability Communication Leading to Sustainable Behaviour; Source: Author.

8.2.3. Strategy

The strategic part treats a sustainability communication fitting to the target group, moreover the people, who are very important for success, and the media and budget planning in general.

Target group fitting Sustainability Communication

To reach the target described above the strategy has to consider the target groups influencing aspects. Further it is essential, regardless of whether the topic is presented subtle or slather, the operators must stand behind their activities. According to this, it is probably especially known by festival operators that those who remain true to their own path earn recognition.

Due to the situation that the general societal opinion is at the festival less important than what the peer group thinks and the *'product characteristics'* of sustainability (behaving sustainable safes environment and climate) alone do not convince anybody to change, communication should be firstly connected with the superficial value orientation of the young adults (see Kroeber-Riel 1988: 25 et seq.).

Emanating from the visitors specific attributes are friendship and also a feeling of cultural solidarity as people are proud to be part of a special event with special acts, especially recognizable by uncountable wall posts at the *facebook* pages of the festivals. In addition, hedonistic values like

96

freedom and enjoyment can be used demonstrating that there is no contradiction between this and sustainable behaviour. Apart from environmentalism there is as well a high potential for including further altruistic values like safety and responsibility (see Wehner 1996: 25). Regarding the festival feeling it is absolutely advisable for SC to emphasize the sustainable solutions rather than sustainable challenges referring to the negative impacts on personal well-being and motivation (see p. 15). Positive advertisement promises incentives in the form of social recognition or money saving opportunities, as they are forceful positive amplifiers (see Hilgard/Bower 1973: 135).

All attendees have in common that they like to go to festivals. But their attitude towards sustainability topics differs a lot as the survey results have shown. The communication measure demands especially to divide between them (see p. 55 et seq.). A lot of visitors' are really interested in and caring for a sustainable development (in the image shortly described as *'eco-oriented'*. They are likely to be open for more information and educational aspects, but have naturally nothing against entertaining aspects.

Then festival fans take part, who do not care or at least do not like to care at all during a festival (*'non-eco-oriented'*), and should not be interested in information or education, unless it is connected to another favourite topic (e. g. in case somebody is a passionate biker). Otherwise they only participate, if they realize any advantage for themselves, what demands indirect sustainability communication underlining entertainment or other incentives (see p. 19 et seq.). The majority are those who cannot be classified in one clear direction, also well described by Meegan Jones:

> "They may not see themselves as 'greenies', but as responsible members of society, caring for the Earth and thinking about the well-being of future generations", (Jones, 20120: 38).

Accordingly, social recognition certainly plays a role. Visibly in the image all three groups influence each other. As sustainability has an image problem, the *'non-eco-oriented'* attendees have a big influence, even if they are by far the smallest group. The *semi-eco-oriented* group do not want to bother themselves with the topic or the measures are either not reliable or just too burdensome. Though, this insists a high potential for direct SC comprising educational as well as informational aspects, when well adequately adapted.

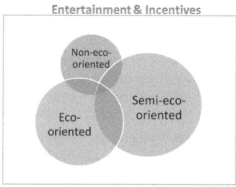

Figure 35: Attitude of Festival Visitors Regarding Sustainability (Cycles not exactly to Scale of Results); Source: Author.

Thus, sustainability communication should not overcharge the mass. To catch the crowd regarding sustainability issues reduction should be designed in an encouraging, not in a menacing way. Beside the advantages for climate and environment, it should also be advertised, which benefits arise for attendees, connected to attributes described above.

For other aspects like carbon offset or background measures, further details have to be easily accessible as transparency moderately presented is an important issue for trust. Meaning that info boards at the showers how many water can be saved due to the adapted technique is interesting, blinking buttons on the website opening the sustainability report or volunteers acting like in a sales promotion rather tend to be counter-productive.

Figure 36: Example of an Information Board at Peats Ridge Festival; Source: Jones 2010: 340.

VIPs for Sustainability:

The people on the party who are definitely able to generate social pressure, are the idols on the stage (see p. 36 et seq.). Operators should try to coordinate those matters in advance. Involvement can be simply generated by integrating a remark about a specific topic in their stage program. Why not ask for applause to thank the regional stall holders caring every day for delicious food? However, discussion rounds or educational activities together with artists are rather feasible at smaller festivals with less prominent bands, but drawing backstage meet-and-greets for instance for car-pooling, shuttle service use or waste collection would be attractive incentives. Also initiated competitions like bicycling for power generation are feasible. Being creative and challenging the festival crowd a bit is a good recipe for reaching sustainability goals.

Beside the artists are the volunteers as well VIPs for SC. Thus, the organizers should select the right ones. At first they must fit to the festival and need as well the same characteristics like good travel guides for a youth trip: easy going, strong-willed, confident and a considerable empathy (see RUF 2012). Apart from caring for sustainability matters, they can also satisfy visitors' desire for safety or provide first aid and support therewith remarkably the so important relaxed atmosphere (see p. 57). It is certainly advisable to appreciate the efforts at least with expense allowance or probably tickets for the following year.

But as mentioned earlier, for real success it is essential that every employee stands behind the idea and is able to give information about it, if attendees ask.

Media and Budget Planning

Self-evidently, it would be preposterous to indicate the budget structure for the media activities. Therefore, the structure of different festivals and demands are too different. But due to the analysed requirements of SC for music festivals, three main media can be examined to transport the message:

Table 4: Main Media for Music Festivals' Sustainability Communication

Print Media	Needed for in advance information brochures or advertisements announcing for instance shuttle services or the new supermarket and during the festival in form of placards or some information material
Online Media	Especially website and social media activities very important due to the web affinity, needed especially for announcing initiatives, calling for participation, distributing news in this field, providing sustainability information (or if already available a sustainability report)
Below-the-line (BTL) communication	Meaning new creative ways of communication apart from classical methods, which like to address target groups personally, without being superficially recognized as advertisement; it includes for festivals especially: • Sponsoring • Promotion teams; meaning for this purpose artists, NGOs and all of the festival team, but particularly volunteers and employees working at the info point • Events: Information and education through visitor involvement activities realized by NGOs • Incentives: Discounts on combined tickets, raffles for meet and greet or permanent rewards like posters/free drinks for full bin bags • Product placement: Including give-aways (e. g. organic shower gel) and products in stalls

8.2.4. Realisation

Ways how to realize sustainability communication adequately to the crowd in the specific fields are demonstrated below. Anyway, there is no warranty made to the extent of completeness.

Framework program: Educational and information activities by NGOs should be arranged in a small scale were curious people can participate in a relaxed atmosphere without standing in the spot light and perceive social pressure by the non-eco-oriented. If it is the first time that NGOs are introduced, one or two initiatives should be enough pursuing a broadly accepted topic. So it is done by *ViVA CON AGUA*, which has successfully participated in many German Festivals (see 2012).

Online:

- Information at websites sustainability part that the festival is glad to have NGO 'xy' at the campsite, presenting their link and brief information about their efforts
- Providing the program items like sport contests (with registration forms) and NGO measure
- Information at the sustainability part of the festival website about replaced unsustainable framework items in favour of more sustainable ones

Print:

- Mainly material from the NGOs
- Topic related placards or art installations close to the NGOs' to support the message

BTL:

- NGO members
- All educational and informational activities
- Any give-aways and incentives due to battles or raffles

A base for controlling are output related KPIs like the amount of participants or new NGO supporters. Outcome related KPIs should be examined as well, what means for instance how many people really want to reduce plastic-, energy- or water-consumption. Those things can be simply questioned at the end of an activity.

Mobility: Giving additional information is also helpful for the promotion of shuttle services, because therewith procedures can be explained and they allay doubts.

Online:

- Information about the shuttles' advantages, including environmental aspects
- Providing details about luggage space, departure times or the possibility to reserve two seats so that friends can sit next to each other

- Publish an info phone numbers for hesitating people and emergency phone numbers for the whole festival dates in case somebody cannot find or take the shuttle or somebody else needs a ride

Print:

- Conspicuous placards for departure places
- Schedules (with emergency numbers) at departure places for shuttles during the festival as well as departure dates for the last day
- Adhesive foils (of course environmental friendly) remarking the festival shuttle service as what they am
- Information material or other festival related reading stuff for the ride

BTL:

- Easy going and reliable driver
- Comfortable and reliable shuttles

KPIs are load factor and request of the shuttles as well as the achieved carbon reductions. Due to its key role and as it is a sensitive topic for the festival fans, main arguments are collected in the table below:

Table 5: Arguments for Sustainable Transport Alternatives

Option 1: Promoting public transport		
Benefits own car use	Solution	Communication Arguments
No big price difference comparing to bus or train (probably cheaper)	Combi- tickets for bus/train and festival with discounts; Discount on festival ticket, if using public transport through cooperation programs; Limitation of car spaces; Fee on car spaces	Saves money; No traffic jam; No driving stress
Independent, in front and during the festival	Reliable departure times and places; Shuttle Service during the event	Arriving right in front of entrance; car cannot be damaged; nobody drives drunken
Storage place for heavy luggage, no need to eliminate	Enough storage place in the shuttles; unload close to the camping ground and offer to purchase camping gear at the event; Supermarket at festival	No heavy luggage; time-saving as no need for an additional shopping tour
Option 2: Promoting lift share		
Benefit of single driving	Solution	Communication Arguments
No complicated arrangements with strangers regarding meeting place, music, temperature	Promoting car-pooling as a typical travel method for the attendees of this festival, a used to be method; Promote it through competitions	Money savings potential and fun factor Contest with lucrative prices and price-giving ceremony

Sale of Goods: For retailers it is advisable to hint at the regional or fair trade background of the products, because they are important aspects for the sample. For organic food, *bio* should not be the main sales argument. Of course a label can be shown in the stalls, but for the main communication it is more advisable to provide faceable facts.

Hence, a conspicuous placement of the farms address and pictures, ideally with the sales person, and information material show that the producer is convinced to care for animals or fruits correctly and rather generate trust. This can be supported by slogans like '*No fake, our sausages are from happy pigs*'. Close to the stalls, placards and installations can be placed, explaining the necessity of organic food, sustainable goods and fair trade. They avoid too many questions for stall holder in the sales process, give answers to those who are interested but do not ask, and calls the attention of those people who do not care for it. Operators can support their stall holders by developing those strategies. A good example fitting to this direction delivers the farmers of www.*meinekleinefarm.org*.

Online:

- Introducing stall holders and providing background information and links to their website
- If a contest for the best sustainability measures took place, publish the winners with pictures of the festivals' award ceremony

Print (mainly due to stall holders):

- Advertising posters with slogans due to fair trade or free-range animals
- Information material about the background conditions

BTL (mainly due to stall holders):

- Open minded employees happy to give detailed information
- Open minded festival crew appreciating on occasion the sustainable production way of their stallholders

KPIs are purchase and request for organic, vegetarian and vegan food as well as a customer increase after the festival ended.

Ticketing: A ticket or share of the ticket to compensate the own emissions and a combi-ticket offering a good price for shuttle and festival entry are the main options to support festivals sustainability measures by ticket purchase:

Online:

- Informing about combination possibilities with shuttle service
- Informing that the festival takes 2 % of the ticket price for carbon compensating measures and publish the supported climate protection initiative on the website with a link to them
- Providing online ticket purchase

Print:

- Naming at tickets the carbon compensating measure (raises attention to it, visitors show it to friends)
- Represent graphically the CO_2- savings comparing to own car at the combi-tickets

KPIs are ticket purchase and also number of additional requests (in case tickets are sold out).

Waste and Water: Campaigns like '*love your tent*' demonstrate how it works to promote a sustainable measure successfully, appealing to empathy of humans. This works as well for the sale of regional products (see Ganzert et al 2004: 26). Hence, the reduction of waste and water should be supported by:

Online:

- Informing about re-usable cups and dishes, tent rental provider and the festival supermarket with prices (transparency!) so that less food gets bought in advance
- Promote that the organising team really dislike left camping gear due to the arising problems
- Asking for bringing own dishes and for using the donation service, if they do not want to keep the tent
- Inform about provision of fresh water for free during the festival
- Strongly promote the supermarket right on the festival as well as its moderate prices

Print:

- Conspicuous placards in a corporate design for the different waste related spots
- Prints on cups informing that they are returnable or reusable
- Information material for the tent donation station, bin bags and personal ashtrays and the need for saving water

- Placards in front of the showers promoting water saving and inform about festivals' water management

BTL:

- Clearly marked different coloured waste bins for easier separation
- Volunteers to provide waste related coloured bin bags, sponsored (ideally by a sustainable business) personal ashtrays and to assist friendly by waste separation and control that nobody vandalizes at the campsite
- Trash mountain visible positioned to create awareness for waste generation
- Invitation of NGOs working in the field of waste and water management
- Organic shower gel and shampoo for free in the showers

The most important KPI is the tonnes of waste. Nevertheless, analysing the use intensity of the single measures like the usage of the provided shower gel or number of people bringing own dishes to the stalls, makes sense to figure out, where communication can be improved.

Horizontal measures: Some SC measures apply for all or several presented categories so that they can be named separately:

Online:

- Printable info guide about options for visitors to behave sustainably in front and during the festival
- Creating a webpage were all information about sustainability measures become published, including improvements and news updates like involvement of new artists
- Asking attendees for improvement hints and further suggestions in front of the festival and afterwards in order to integrate them

Print

- Advertisement in music or lifestyle magazines, which includes measures like combi-tickets or the tent-rental station
- Information boards wherever improvements were achieved for instance for energy efficiency measures

BTL

- Artists talking about sustainability initiatives
- Volunteers informing about sustainability initiative, if they were asked

- Provision of a festival supermarket with moderate prices (reducing food purchase in advance so that shuttle service becomes attractive for more visitors and less waste arises by still wrapped, not consumed food)

General KPIs, which are finally important to know, are number or share of positive and negative reactions per personal contact, mail at the online forum regarding the SC as well as measurable and recognizable reactions of other stakeholders (e. g. media releases).

9. Conclusion

Finished going through this paper, the reader has explored three dominant topics, totally different and each of these detailing in numerous aspects.

Sustainability itself is, despite its long history and its current demands, distinguished by discordance and slow motions. In order to achieve the needed change for sustainable development, the strong sustainability approach must be assumed and corresponding behaviour has to become adapted by the society. Above that people should be able to be self-sufficient in case prosperity lacks arise due to resource scarcity. Here, economy can play a key role.

Festivals are an important and increasing part of the music entertainment branch, and an established mass event, especially for young adults. But compared to the beginnings, their meanings have totally changed. Attendees want to let go and feel free without any compromises. However, the majority of them do think, as the most of the German society, that environmentalism is very important. Nonetheless, there are great differences referring to the willingness to change used traditions during the festival visit. But without audience participation sustainability measures of operators cannot unfold its potentials.

That is the point where sustainability communication becomes essential. As an enhancement of environmental communications, due to the Rio Summit, it includes in communication the involvement of individuals as the affected and influencing actors. But SC in business and public are broadly seen as different activities, so that till now the most businesses barely contribute to fostering sustainable behaviour among citizens. Due to this general perception no further incentives arise to act above the CSR initiatives, which are promising the license to operate. Thus, executives feel no pressure to change their business case into sustainable compatible ones.

In the case of music festival operators, a customer encouraging SC strategy was quite interesting, not only if they are altruistic and image driven. It can help for instance to reduce waste and to save water, which in turn reduces costs. Above that many festival have already overtaken responsibility for further sustainability aspects like promoting public audience travel.

This engagement goes in line with their customers, as more and more demand a responsible management, deciding where to go with their wallets. The broad mass stands behind those measures and is willing to support it. One third would even be interested in learning practical things for sustainable development during the festival. But those, who are hesitating due to social pressure, convenience, general reluctance or insecurity to take the shuttles, keeping the campsite tidy or just to buy organic food, need a nudge. Hence, the sustainability communication strategy must consider their needs and slightly push them in the desired direction.

Setting adequate incentives, encouraging the crew and actors to support the festivals targets and make the single topics accessible with an attractive and transparent communication fitting to the crowds needs, the SC strategy has the chance to unfold its whole potential. Therefore, the establishment of a central unit to manage these purposes is recommendable.

Finally, SC measures could greatly contribute to the improvement of the sustainability performance of the festival, what can be proudly communicated to other interested stakeholders refining their public image. They are further able to participate in re-creating events by the contents rather than by sensual overloads. Thereby, they contribute in the rising of the needed awareness for sustainable development among the young generation, who are becoming more attentive customers.

Moreover, festivals can earn back something of their original spirit, to depart from the common beaten societal track by taking true responsibility for the future, and inspiring the whole event branch as well and probably some other branches, too.

BIBLIOGRAPHY

Agenda 21 (1992): Changing consumption patterns, 4.1 - 4.27, UNCED, Rio de Janeiro, URL [05.02.2012]: http://www.un.org/esa/dsd/agenda21/res_agenda21_04.shtml.

AGFA (2011): Applying for the Award 2011, URL [10.11.11]: http://www.agreenerfestival.com/2011/01/applying-for-the-greener-festival-award-2011/.

AGFA (2012a): Environmental Self- Assessment Form, URL [05.02.2012]: http://www.agreenerfestival.com/wp-content/uploads/downloads/AGFA2012_SELFASSESSMENT_FINAL.pdf.

AGFA (2012b): Home, URL [06.03.2012]: http://www.agreenerfestival.com.

Alcott, B. (2008). "The sufficiency strategy: Would rich-world frugality lower environmental impact?" Ecological Economics, 64, pp. 770-786.

Allen, T.F.H., J.A. Tainter & T. W. Hoekstra (2003). Supply-Side Sustainability. New York: Columbia University Press.

Allen, T.F.H. (2009)."Hierarchy Theory in Ecology". In S.E. Jørgensen (Ed.) Ecosystem Ecology, Amsterdam, Boston: Academic Press, Elsevier, pp.114-120.

Altobelli, C. F. (2007): Marktforschung: Methoden - Anwendungen – Praxisbeispiele. Utb Gmbh, 2nd edition, Stuttgart.

Antes, R. (1992): Die Organisation des betrieblichen Umweltschutzes. In: Ulrich, S. (Ed.): Handbuch des Umweltmanagements. C. H. Beck. Munich, pp. 487–509.

Arte (2008): Green Touring, 29.11.2008, 03.00 am, 52 min., Tracks, Germany, URL: [06.03.2012]: http://www.arte.tv/de/2326990,CmC=2326850.html.

Badi, U. (2011): Tainter's law: where is the physics?, URL: [03.03.2012]: http://cassandralegacy.blogspot.com/2011/03/tainters-law-where-is-physics.html.

Bauer, S. (2008): Leitbild der nachhaltigen Entwicklung in: Information zur politischen Bildung, Heft 287 (überarbeitete Neuauflage), Bundeszentrale für Politische Bildung, Bonn.

BCF (2011): Car Pooling. URL [30.11.2011]: http://www.bigchill.net/festival/info/green-0.

Bellinghausen, R. (2007): Die ökonomischen und touristischen Effekte von Music Festivals, 1st Edition, GRIN Verlag, Norderstedt.

Berger, P. L./Luckmann, T. (1966): The Social Construction of Reality. A Treatise in the Sociology of Society as a Human Product, Knowledge, Garden City, New York: Anchor Books, pp. 51- 66.

Belz, F.-M./Bilharz, M.(2005): Nachhaltiger Konsum: Zentrale Herausforderung für moderne Verbraucherpolitik. Consumer Science. Diskussionsbeitrag Nr.1. Munich.

Beitsch, M./Huth, N./Arenz, R.(2011): Netzgesellschaft. Eine repräsentative Untersuchung zur Mediennutzung und dem Informationsverhalten der Gesellschaft in Deutschland. BITKOM Bundesverband Informationswirtschaft, Telekommunikation und neue Medien e. V., Berlin.

Bieber, A. (2007): "Live Earth"Al Gore organisiert Mega-Livekonzert für Klimaschutz. SPIEGEL ONLINE, 15.02.2007, URL [06.03.2012]: http://www.spiegel.de/kultur/musik/0,1518,466600,00.html.

Blake Alcott, „The sufficiency strategy: Would rich-world frugality lower environmental impact?", Ecological Economics.

Blanke, M./Hüttenrauch, I. (2012): Press Release: Startschuss für das Rocken am Brocken Festival 2012, 21/01/2012. URL [16/02/2012]: http://www.pr-inside.com/de/startschuss-f-r-das-rocken-am-b-r3011420.htm.

BMU (2007): Forsa-Umfrage zu "Biologische Vielfalt", Stand: Mai 2007, URL [13.10.2011]: http://www.bmu.de/naturschutz_biologische_vielfalt/internationaler_naturschutz/uebereinkommen_ueber_die_biologische_vielfalt/doc/print/39399.php.

BMU (2010): Umweltbewusstsein in Deutschland 2010 Ergebnisse einer repräsentativen Bevölkerungsumfrage, 1st edition, Dessau Roßlau.

Böhm, F. (1966): Privatrechtsgesellschaft und Marktwirtschaft, ORDO 17er Band, pp. 75- 102.

Bottrill, C./Liveman, D./Boykoff, M. (2008): Carbon soundings: greenhouse gas emissions of the UK music industry. Environmental Research letter 5, IOP Publishing, Bristol, pp.

Boulding, K. E- (1966): The Economics of the Coming Spaceship Earth, New York.

Boulding, K. E. (1970). A Primer in Social Dynamics, New York: Free Press.

Bowdin, G./Allen, J./O'Toole, W./Harris, R./ McDonnell, I. (2010): Event Management, 3rd edition, A Butterworth-Heinemann Title, Burlington.

Briceno T./Stagl, S. (2006): The role of social processes for sustainable consumption. Journal of Cleaner Production, 14, pp. 1541-1551.

Brown, P.M/Cameron, L.D. (2000): What can be done to reduce overconsumption?. Ecological Economics, 32, pp 27-41.

Buchmann, S.L./Nabhan, G.P. (1996): The forgotton pollinators, Island Press, Washington D.C., pp. 292.

Carlowitz, H. C. v. (1713): Sylvicultura Oeconomica, Haußwirthliche Nachricht und Naturmäßige Anweisung zur Wilden Baum-Zucht, pp. 105-113.

CASSE (2011): Definition, URL [10.10.2011]: http://steadystate.org/discover/definition/.

CF (2011): Car-Pooling. URL [27.11.2011]: http://www.coachella.com/festival-info/sustainability.

Clausen, J./Fichter, K. (1996): Umweltbericht – Umwelterklärung. Praxis glaubwürdiger Kommunikation von Unternehmen, München/Wien: Hanser Verlag.

CN (2011): Framework Program. URL [02.12.2011]: http://www.croissantneuf.co.uk/.

Colin, 2011: Bäume für Konzerte, Musikstars für die Umwelt, Green Biz, Musikmarkt – Das Branchenmagazin, 13/2011, Munich. Pp. 6-11.

Common, M. (2007). "Measuring national economic performance without using prices", Ecological Economics, 64 (1): 92-102.

COP 6 (2002): Strategic Plan for the Convention on Biological Diversity, Decision VI/26, URL [05.02.2012]: http://www.cbd.int/decision/cop/?id=7200.

Daly, H. (1996). Beyond Growth. Beacon Press, Boston.

Degener, S. (Ed.)(2009): International Motorcycle Symposium 2009, German Insurance Association, Berlin.

DeSombre, E. R. (2006): Global Environmental Institutions, London/New York.

DGAP-Media (2011): Q-Cells SE: Melt!-Festival setzt mit Q-Cells auf Solarenergie, 15.07.2011, URL [16.12.2011]: http://www.finanznachrichten.de/nachrichten-2011-07/20799965-q-cells-se-melt-festival-setzt-mit-q-cells-auf-solarenergie-015.htm.

Diamond, J. (2005): Collapse. How Societies Choose to Fail or Succeed. New York: Viking Penguin.

Diller, H. (2001): Kommunikationspolitik; in: Diller, H. (Hrsg.): Vahlens Großes Marketing Lexikon, 2nd Edition, München: Beck/Vahlen, pp. 791-793.

Dinkel, F. (2010): Von der Expo 02 zur Euro 08. In: Praktischer Umweltschutz Schweiz Pusch (Ed.) (2010): Umweltschutz bei Sportanlässen, Stadtfesten und Open Airs. 2/2010, pp. 16-18.

Doble, M./Kruthiventi, A.K. (eds.)(2007): Green Chemistry & Engineering, Academic Press, Elsevier, Amsterdam.

Dryzek, J.G. (2005). The Politics of the Earth. Oxford : Oxford University Press.

EC (2011): Wasser. Wege zum erfolgreichen Betrieb, URL [20.11.2011]: http://ecocamping.net/18645/Campingunternehmer/Tipps-und-Infos/Wege-zu-einem-erfolgreichen-Betrieb/Wasser/index.aspx.

EFA (2012): And the winners are!. URL [16/02/2012]: http://eu.festivalawards.com/news/and-the-winners-are/.

FB (2011a): Glastonbury facebook page. URL [05.3.2012]: https://www.facebook.com/glastonburyofficial

FF (2011a): Sustainability. URL [29.11.2011]: http://2011.fallsfestival.com.au/sustainability/.

FF (2011b): Sustainability Report 2010. URL [06.03.2012]: http://2011.fallsfestival.com.au/wp-content/uploads/2011/07/Falls_Sustainabilty_web.pdf.

Fichter, K. (2000): Umweltkommunikation und Wettbewerbsfähigkeit; in: Fichter, K./Schneidewind, U. (Ed.): Umweltschutz im globalen Wettbewerb. Neue Spielregeln für das grenzenlose Unternehmen; Berlin: Springer-Verlag, pp. 263-276.

Freeling, N. (2011): Earth Overshoot Day 2011, Global Footprint Network, URL [03.03.2012]: http://www.footprintnetwork.org/press/EODay_Media_Backgrounder_2011.pdf.
Galler, F./Rost, N. (2011): Solidarökonomischer Aufbruch der Region Berchtesgardener Land, in:

Fritz, P./Huber, J./Levi, H.-W. (Hrsg.)(1995): Nachhaltigkeit in naturwissenschaftlicher und sozialwissenschaftlicher Perspektive (S. 31- 46). Stuttgart: S. Hirzel - Wissenschaftliche Verlagsgesellschaft.

Ganzert, C./Burdick, B./Scherhorn, G. (2004): Empathie, Verantwortlichkeit, Gemeinwohl: Versuch über die Selbstbehauptungskräfte der Region, Wuppertal Institute, Wuppertal.

Elsen, S. (2011): Ökosoziale Transformation. Solidarische Ökonomie und die Gestaltung des Gemeinwesens, 1st edition 2011, AG SPAK Bücher, Neu-Ulm.

Geiser, K. (2001). Materials Matter. Toward a Sustainable Materials Policy. Cambridge, Mass: The MIT Press.

Georgescu-Roegen, N. (1971): The Entropy Law and the Economic Process. Harvard University Press, Cambridge/Massachusetts.

Gershuny, J. (1983). Social Innovation and the Division of Labour. Oxford: Oxford University Press.

Getz, D. (1999). The impacts of mega events on tourism: Strategies for destinations In Andersson, T. D., C. Persson, B. Sahlberg, & L. Strom, (Ed.), *The Impact of Mega Events*. (pp.5-32). Ostersund, Sweden: European Tourism Research Institute.

GfK (2007): GfK-Studie zum Konsumverhalten der Konzert- und Veranstaltungsbesucher in Deutschland, ed. by idkv und Musikmarkt, Munich.

GF (2011a): Greenpeace field, URL [21.11.2011]: http://www.glastonburyfestivals.co.uk/areas/the-green-fields/the-greenpeace-field).

GF (2011b): Green trader award winners. URL [01.12.2011]: http://www.glastonburyfestivals.co.uk/news/green-trader-awards-winners.

GF (2011c): Homepage. URL [29.11.2011]: http://www.glastonburyfestivals.co.uk/.

GF (2011d): What you can do, URL [29.11.2011]: http://www.glastonburyfestivals.co.uk/information/green-glastonbury/what-you-can-do.

GF (2011e): Shuttle Service, URL [10.12.2011]: http://www.glastonburyfestivals.co.uk/Information/getting-here/by-bus.

GF (2011f): By Car. URL [10.12.2011]: (http://www.glastonburyfestivals.co.uk/information/getting-here/by-car.

GMI (2011): Greener Catering, URL [30.11.2011]: http://www.greenmusicinitiative.de/best-practise/greener-catering-at-festivals/).

GMI (2012): News, URL [06.03.2012]: http://www.agreenerfestival.com/.

Gminder, C. U. (2005): Nachhaltigkeitsstrategien systemisch umsetzen. Eine qualitative Exploration der Organisationsaufstellung als Managementmethode, D I S S E R T A T I O N der Universität St. GallenSpescha D-Druck, St.Gallen.

Godemann, J./Michelsen, G. (2011)(Ed.): Sustainability Communication: Interdisciplinary Perspectives and Theoretical Foundations, Springer Science and Business Media, Dordrecht, Heidelberg, London, New York.

GP (2010): In the picture at the Thames Festival, 11.09.2010, London, URL [27.11.2011]: http://www.flickr.com/photos/48242091@N07/4993675308/in/pool-1503481@N22/lightbox/.

GR (2010): Newsletter for Stakeholder. June 2010, Festival Republic, URL [29.11.2011]: http://www.dcsiteservices.com/files/greenRepublicNewsletterJune2010_smaller_v2010.0.3.pdf.

Graf, C. (1995): Kulturmarketing. Open Air und populäre Musik. Dt. Universitätsverlag, Wiesbaden.

Griffiths, J. (2010): Making the business case for corporate action on ecosystems, forum CSR International, 2010, International Network for Environmental Management, Munich, 17.

Grosse, F. (2010): Is Recycling 'Part of the Solution? The Role of Recycling in an Expanding Society and a World of Finite Resources. Sapiens, Vol.3, N°1. URL [05.10.2011]: thttp://sapiens.revues.org/index906.html.

Grunenberg, H./Kuckartz U. (2005): Umweltbewusstsein. Empirische Erkenntnisse und Konsequenzen für die Nachhaltigkeitskommunikation. In: Michelsen, G./Godemann, J.(Ed.)(2005): Handbuch Nachhaltigkeitskommunikation, oekom Verlag, München, p. 195- 206.

Grunwald, A. (Ed.)(2003): Technikgestaltung zwischen Wunsch und Wirklichkeit, Springer, Berlin.

GV (2011): Eco Village. URL [27.11.2011]: http://greenvillage.ie/2011/09/eco-village-line-up/.

Haldern Pop (2012), URL [05.03.2012]: http://www.haldern-pop.de/de/festival/geschichte.

Hamm, H./Jerger, I. (2011): Grün gewinnt, in: natur + kosmos, december 2011, Konradin Meiden GmbH, Leinfelden- Echterdingen, pp.: 12- 20.

Hardtke, A./Prehn, M. (2001): Perspektiven der Nachhaltigkeit. Vom Leitbild zur Erfolgsstrategie, Wiesbaden.

Harvey, D. (1990). The Condition of Postmodernity. Cambridge, MA. And London, Blackwell.

Hauff, V. (Ed.)(1987): Our Common Future. Brundtland Report, from the United Nations World Commission on Environment and Development (WCED), Eggenkamp Verlag, Greven.

Harvey, M. A. et al. (2001). "Between Demand & Consumption: A Framework for Research." CRIC Discussion paper N°40. University of Manchester.

Hawken, P./Lovins, A. B./Lovins, L. H.(1999). Natural Capitalism. The Next Industrial Revolution, Earthscan, London.

Hebbel-Seeger, A./Förster, J. (Editors)(2008): Eventmanagement und Marketing im Sport. Emozionale Erlebnisse und kommerzieller Erfolg.

Hennicke, P. (2002). Effizienz und Suffizienz in einem System nachhaltiger Energienutzung. In M. Linz (Hrsg.), *Von nichts zu viel: Suffizienz gehört zur Zukunftsfähigkeit: Über ein Arbeitsvorhabendes Wuppertal Instituts* (S. 57-70): Wuppertal Institut für Klima, Umwelt, Energie.

Herring, H./Sorrell, S. (eds.) (2009): Energy Efficiency and Sustainable Consumption. The Rebound Effect, Palgrave McMillan, Basingstoke.

Hilgart, E. R./Bower, G. H. (1973): Theorien des Lernens I und II, Ernst- Klett- Verlag, Stuttgart.

Hirsch, F. (1976): Social Limits to Growth. Routledge and Kegan, London/Henley.

Huber, J. (1995). Nachhaltige Entwicklung durch Suffizienz, Effizienz und Konsistenz. In P. Fritz, J. Huber, H.W. Levi (Ed): Nachhaltigkeit in naturwissenschaftlicher und sozialwissenschaftlicher Perspektive, Wissenschaftliche Verlagsgesellschaft/Edition Universitas, Stuttgart.

Ifak Institut (2009): Welche Verkehrsmittel haben Sie bei Ihrer letzten Haupturlaubsreise der letzten 12 Monate benutzt?, Typologie der Wünsche, Media Markt Analysen, URL [20.02.2012]: http://de.statista.com/statistik/daten/studie/174497/umfrage/auf-letzter-haupturlaubsreise-benutzte-verkehrsmittel.

IoWF (2011): Love your tent campaign. URL [01.12.2011]: http://www.isleofwightfestival.com/love-your-tent.aspx.

IPCC (2007a): Working Group I: Couplings Between Changes in the Climate System and Biogeochemistry, Fourth Assessment Report: Climate Change 2007, Geneva.

IPCC (2007b): Working Group II: Impacts, Adaptation and Vulnerability, Fourth Assessment Report: Climate Change 2007, Geneva.
IUCN (1980), World Conservation Strategy, URL [04.10.2011]: http://data.iucn.org/dbtw-wpd/edocs/WCS-004.pdf.

Jackson, T. (2009). Prosperity Without Growth. Economics for a Finite Planet. Earthscan, London.

Jänicke, M. (2008). Ecological modernisation: new perspectives. Journal of Cleaner Production. 16, 557-565.

Jakob, N./Schoen, H.,/Zerback, T.(Hrsg.)(2009): Sozialforschung im Internet. Methodologie und Praxis der Online-Befragung, VS Verlag für Sozialwissenschaften, Wiesbaden.

Japp , K. P. (2000): Risiko, transcript Verlag, Bielefeld.

JB (2012): about JB, URL [06.03.2012]: http://www.juliesbicycle.com/about-jb.

Jossè, H./Stobbe, R./Kuhn, P. (2011): Controlling der Maerktingkommunikation, DPRG/Universität Leipzig, Berlin/Leipzig.

Kals, E./Maes, J. (2002): Sustainable development and emotions. In Schmuck, P./Schultz, W.P. (ediors): Psychology of sustainable development, Norwell, MA: Kluwer Academic, 97-122.

Kaletta, B. (2008): Anerkennung oder Abwertung: Über die Verarbeitung sozialer Desintegration, 1st edition, VW Verlag für Sozialwissenschaftn, Wiesbaden.

Kasser, T. (2002). The High Price of Materialism. Cambridge Mass. the MIT Press.
Keynes, J. M. (1930): Economic possibilities for our grandchildren, Essays in Persuasion, Macmillan, London.
Kolm, S.C. (1984). La bonne économie: la réciprocité générale. Paris : PUF.

Koschnick, W. J. (1995): Standard- Lexikon für Markt- und Konsumforschung. Volume 1: A - K. Band, Schäffer-Poeschel Verlag, Stuttgart.

Korhonen, J. (2005). Theory of industrial ecology: the case of the concept of diversity. Progress in Industrial Ecology - An International Journal, 2, pp. 35-72.

Kroeber-Riel, W. (1988): Kommunikation im Zeitalter der Informationsüberlastung. In: Marketing ZFP, 10. Jg., Nb. 3, pp. 182-189.

Krugman, P. (2009): Increasing Returns in a comparative advantage world, Princeton University, URL [03.03.2012]: http://www.princeton.edu/~pkrugman/deardorff.pdf.

Kruse , L. (2005): Nachhaltigkeitskommunikation – Eine psychologische Perspektive. In: Michelsen, G./Godemann, J.(Ed.)(2005): Handbuch Nachhaltigkeitskommunikation, oekom Verlag, München, S. 109–120.

Kuckartz, U./ Ebert, T./Rädiker, S./Stefer, C. (2009): Evaluation online: Internetgestützte Befragung in der Praxis, VS Verlag für Sozialwissenschaften, Wiesbaden.

Lazarsfeld, P./Berelson, B./Gaudet, H.: The People's Choice. How the Voter Makes up his Mind in a Presidential Campaign. Columbia University Press, 3rd edition, London/New York.

Lee, C.-K./Lee, Y.- K./Wills, B. E. (2003): Segmentation of festival motivation by nationality and satisfaction, Tourism Management, Pergamont.

Leitzmann, C./Beck, A./Hamm, U./Hermanowski, R. (2009): Praxishandbuch Bio-Lebensmittel, Volume 1, Behr's Verlag, Hamburg.

Léopold, G. (2011): One Planet Events - Methodology and tools to green your events?. WWF International, URL [16.12.2011]: http://wwf.panda.org/how_you_can_help/live_green/at_the_office/green_events/.

LF (2012): Cub Deposits. URL [06.02.2012]: http://www.latitudefestival.co.uk/info/category/food_and_drink.

LiB (2011a): Free Water Initiative, URL [01.12.2012]: http://lightninginabottle.org/environment/free-water/.

Lichtl, M. (2003): Umwelt. Get the kick, In: PÖ 63/64, Munich.

Lintott, J. (2007): Sustainable consumption and sustainable welfare. In Zaccaï, E. (Ed.)(2007): Sustainable Consumption, Ecology and Fair Trade. London and New York: Routledge. pp. 41-57.

Lucas, R. (2007): Zukunftsfähiges Eventmarketing: Strategien, Instrumente, Beispiele; Kultur Kommerz 14, Erich Schmidt Verlag, Berlin.

Lucas, R. (2008): Kreisläufe schließen. Die Renaissance der Regionen In: Sachs (Ed.)(2008):Zukunftsfähiges Deutschland in einer globalisierten Welt, 2nd Edition, pp. 19- 32.

Lucas, R./Matys, T. (2003): Erlebnis Nachhaltigkeit? Möglichkeiten und Grenzen des Eventmarketing bei der Vermittlung gesellschaftlicher Werte. Wuppertal Papers, Nb. 136, Wuppertal.

Lucas, R./Wilts, H. (2004): „Events für Nachhaltigkeit" – ein neues Geschäftsfeld für die Eventwirtschaft?. Wuppertal Papers, Nb. 149, Wuppertal.

Luther, S./Giljum, S. (2010): The material basis of the global economy Worldwide patterns of resource extraction, SERI fact Sheet, Sustainable Europe Research Institute, Vienna, p. 1.

Manno, J. (2002). Commoditization: Consumption Efficiency and an Economy of Care and Connection" in Prinzen, T. M. Maniates and K. Conca (eds), Confronting Consumption. Cambridge, Mass.: the MIT Press., pp. 67-101.

Martens, D. (2011): Spendenwesen: Der Appell ans Gewissen kann auf die Nerven gehen, Der Tagesspiegel, 18.08.2011 14:23 Uhr, URL [13.10.2011]: http://www.tagesspiegel.de/berlin/spendenwesen-der-appell-ans-gewissen-kann-auf-die-nerven-gehen/4508280.html.

Mast C./Fiedler, K.(2005): Nachhaltige Unternehmenskommunikation. In: Michelsen, G./Godemann, J.(Ed.)(2005): Handbuch Nachhaltigkeitskommunikation, oekom Verlag, München, S. 565-576.

Matthies, E./Homberger, I./Matthäus, S./Engelke, P./Moczek, N.(2004): Lokale Agenda- Prozesse psychologisch steuern, Frankfurt a. M.

Max-Neef, M. (1991): Human Scale Development. The Apex Press, New-York/London.

McDonough W. & M. Braungart (2002). Cradle To Cradle. North Point Press, New York.

Meadows, D. H./Randers, J./Meadows, D. (1972): The Limits of Growth. A Report for The Club of Rome's Project on the Predicament of Mankind, Club of Rome, Universe Books, New York.

Meffert, H./Kirchgeorg, M. (1998): Marktorientiertes Umweltmanagement, 3. Edition, Schäffer-Poeschel, Stuttgart.

Meiländer, D. (2011): Unbewusst nachhaltig. Spezial: Mittelstandsfinanzierung, Handelsblatt 08.12.2011, Nb. 238, Köln.

Meinshausen, M. (2008): Eine kurze Anmerkung zu 2°C- Trajektorien, in: Ott, H. E. und Heinrich Böll Foundation (Ed.): Wege aus der Klimafalle, Munich.

Melt! (2011a): M!eco. URL [29.11.2011]: http://www.meltfestival.de/meco/.

Melt! (2011b): M!eco Mobilität. URL [30.11.2011]: http://www.meltfestival.de/meco/?page_id=8.

Michelsen, G. (2005): Nachhaltigkeitskommunikation: Verständnis – Entwicklung - Perspektiven, in: Michelsen, G./Godemann, J. (Ed.): Handbuch Nachhaltigkeitskommunikation: Grundlagen und Praxis. Oekom Verlag, Munich, pp. 25-41.

Millennium Ecosystem Assessment (2005): Ecosystems and Human Well-Being: Synthesis. Island Press, Washington.
Milner, H. V./Keohane, R.O. (1996): Internationalization and Domestic Politics. An Introduction. In: Keohane, R. O./Milner, H.V. (Ed.): Internationalization and Domestic Politics, Cambridge University Press, 3-24, Cambridge.

Mortsiefer, H. (2010): Red Bulls PR-Motor für Extremsportler. Der Tagesspiegel, 14.11.2010, URL [27.11.2011]: http://www.tagesspiegel.de/wirtschaft/sponsoring-red-bulls-pr-motor-fuer-extremsportler/2324162.html.

MSD (2011): Infos. URL [01.12.2011]: http://msdockville.de/infos.

Mummendey H.-D. (1995): Psychologie der Selbstdarstellung. 2nd Revised Edition, Hogrefe, Verlag für Psychologie, Bielefeld.

Navitron (2007): Big Green Gathering. Entry from Mike N., Renewable Energy and Sustainability Forum, URL [010.12.2011]: http://navitron.org.uk/forum/index.php?topic=1791.0.

Nicholson, R./Pearce, D. G. (2001): Why do people attend events: A comparative analysis of visitor motivations at four south island events. Journal of Travel Research, 39, pp. 449-460.

Nørgård, J.S. (2006): Consumer Efficiency in conflict with GDP growth. Ecological Economics 57 15-29.

Norton, B.G. (2005). Sustainability. A Philosophy of Adaptive Ecosystem Management. Chicago and London: Chicago University Press.

O'Neill, C. (2009): Green Shoots, European Festival Report, IQ, Q 4.

Ofstad, S. (Ed.) (1994) Symposium: Sustainable Consumption. Ministry of the Environment, Oslo.

Ostrom, E. (2007). Sustainable socio-ecological systems: an impossibility? Annual Meeting of the American Association for the Advancement of Science, Science and Technology for Sustainable Well-Being, San-Francisco, pp.15–19.

Ostrom, E. (2009). A General Framework for Analyzing Sustainability of Social-Ecological Systems. Science Vol. 325, N°24, pp.419-422.

Ott, K./Muraca, B./Baatz, C. (2011): Strong Sustainability as a Frame for Sustainability Communication, in Godemann, J./Michelsen, G. (2011)(Editors): Sustainability Communication: Interdisciplinary Perspectives and Theoretical Foundations, Springer Science and Business Media, Dordrecht, Heidelberg, London, New York, pp. 13-16.

Oxfam Media Unit (2007): Over 70,000 people count at Glastonbury 2007. 27.07.2007, URL [20.11.2011]: http://www.oxfam.org.uk/applications/blogs/pressoffice/2007/06/27/over-70000-people-count-at-glastonbury-2007/?v=newsblog).

Paech, N. (2005): Nachhaltigkeit zwischen ökologischer Konsistenz und Dematerialisierung: Hat sich die Wachstumsfrage erledigt?, in: Natur und Kultur 6 / 1, 2005, pp. 52- 72.

Paech, N. (2009): The Economy in the Aftermath of Growth, Oldenburg Centre for Sustainability Economics and Management, EINBLICKE, Nb. 49, pp. 24-27.

Paech, N. (2010): Wachsen, in Zukunftsfähiges Hamburg. Zeit zum Handeln. Study of Wuppertale Institute, Munich/Hamburg, pp. 213-241.

Pape, D./Cavelius, A./Ilies, A. (2012): Schlank im Schlaf Vegetarisch, GRÄFE UND UNZER Verlag, München.

Pepels, W. (2005): Marketing- Kommunikation. Werbung. Marken. Medien, 1st edition, Rinteln, Merkur-Verlag.

Perman, R./Ma, Y./Common, M./Maddison, D./McGilvray, J. (2003): Natural Resource and Environmental Economics, 3rd edition, Financial Times/Prentice Hall, Person Education Limited, Glasgow.

Perman, R./Ma, Y./McGilvray, J./Common, M. (2003): Natural Resource and Environmental Economics, 3rd edition, Person Educatoin Limited, Harlow.

PF (2011): Organic food. URL [30.11.2011]: http://www.peatsridgefestival.com.au/sustainability/organic-food.

Pfleiderer, M. (2008): Live- Veranstaltungen von populärer Musik und ihre Rezeption. In Gensch, G./Stöckler, E. M./Tschmuck, P. (Ed.)(2008): Musikrezeption, Musikdistribution und Musikproduktion. Der Wandel des Wertschöpfungsnetzwerkes in der Musikwirtschaft. Gabler Edition Musikwirtschaft, 1st Edition, Wiesbaden.

Phase2 (2012): What is strong sustainability?. The strong Sustainability Think Tank, URL [07.12.2012]: http://nz.phase2.org/what-is-strong-sustainability.

Princen, T. (2003): Principles for Sustainability: From Cooperation and Efficiency to Sufficiency. Global Environment Politics. 3 (1), pp. 33-50.

Princen, T. (2005): The Logic of Sufficiency. MIT Press, Cambridge.

Q-Set (2012): Anleitung. URL [20.02.2012]: http://www.q-set.de/Anleitung/Anleitung.php.

Rawls, J. (1971): A Theory of Justice, The Belknap Press of Harvard University Press.

Reisch, L./Spash, C . L./Bietz, S. (2008): Sustainable Consumption and mass communication; a german experiment, Socieo- Economics and the Environment in Discussion, CSIRO Working Paper Series 2008-12, Clayton South.

RF (2011): Rothbury: What goes where???, URL [07.12.2011]: http://www.rothburyfestival.com/assets/WhatGoesWherebillboard.pdf.

Rheinländer, K./Antes, R./Fiedler, K. (2011): Die nachhaltigkeitsorientiere Kommunikation in Social Media, in UWF, Volume 19, Numbers 1-2, Heidelberg, pp. 95-100.

Ricardo, D. (1817): Principles of Political Economy and Taxation, Everyman, London.

Ricciardi, V. (2008): The Psychology of Risk: The Behavioral Finance Perspective. In: Frank J. FABOZZI (Ed.)(2008): Handbook Of Finance. Volume 2: Investment Management And Financial Management. Wiley, pp. 85–111.

RK (2011): Homepage, URL [20.11.2011]: http://www.rheinkultur.com.

Rogall, H. (2004): Ökonomie der Nachhaltigkeit - Handlungsfelder für Politik und Wirtschaft, Wiesbaden, pp. 127-128.

RUF (2012): Betreuung – Ausbildung in der RUF Akademie, URL [01.03.2012]: http://www.ruf-jugendreisen.de/info/winter/elterninformation-betreuung.asp.

Sachs, W. (2008): Einleitung. In: Sachs (Ed.)(2008):Zukunftsfähiges Deutschland in einer globalisierten Welt, 2nd Edition, pp. 19- 32.

Sachs, W. (2008): Ökologischer Wohlstand, in: Sachs (Ed.)(2008): Zukunftsfähiges Deutschland in einer globalisierten Welt, 2nd Edition, pp. 216- 249.

Sachverständigenrat für Umweltfragen (SRU)(2002): Umweltgutachten 2002 des Rates von Sachverständigen für Umweltfragen. Für eine Neue Vorreiterrolle, Deutscher Bundestag printed matter 14/8792, 14th legislative period, Stuttgart.

Sarkis, A. (20120): Das billige Erdöl ist verbraucht. In: Gresh, A./Radvanyi, J./Rekacewicz, P. (ed)(2010): Atlas der Globalisierung, Le Monde diplomatique/taz, Paris/Berlin, pp. 78-79.

Schemel, H.-J. (2010): Wirtschaftsdiktatur oder Demokratie? Wider dem globalem Standortwettbewerb – für eine weltweite Regionalisierung. Publik Forum, Oberursel.

Scherhorn, G. (1997): Revision des Gebrauchs. In: Schmidt Bleek, F. (Ed.): Ökointelligentes Produzieren und Konsumieren.: Birkenhäuser Verlag, Basel, pp.25- 55.

Schettkat, R. (2009): Analyzing Rebound Effects. Wuppertal Papers N°177, Wuppertal Institute.

Schmidbauer, K./Knödler-Bunte, E. (2004): Das Kommunikationskonzept. Konzepte entwickeln und präsentieren. University press, UMC Potsdam, 1st Edition, Potsdam.

Schnell, R./Hill, P. B./Esser, E. (2011): Methoden der empirischen Sozialforschung. 6th Edition, Munich/Wien/Oldenbourg.

Scholz, R. W. (1996). Effektivität, Effizienz und Verhältnismäßigkeit als Kriterien der Altlastenbearbeitung. URL [23.11.2011]: http://ecollection.ethbib.ethz.ch/show?type=incoll&nr=473 [12.7.2005].

Schor, J. (1998): The Overspent American: Upscaling, Downshifting and the New Consumer. New York: Basic Books.

Schrader (2011): Eine andere Zukunft ist möglich, 09.10.2011 19:48, URL [07.03.2012]: http://www.njuuz.de/beitrag13459.html.

Schuetz, E. (2009): Fun and Free Water at the Vermont Brewers' Festival., Blog 27.07.2009, URL [01.12.2012]: http://www.foodandwaterwatch.org/blogs/fun-and-free-water-at-the-vermont-brewers-festival/.

Schulze, G. (1992): Die Erlebnisgesellschaft. Kultursoziologie der Gegenwart. Frankfurt am Main.

Schulze, G. (2000): Kulissen des Glücks – Streifzüge durch die Eventkultur. Frankfurt am Main/New York.

Schumpeter, J. (1942): Capitalism, Socialism, Democracy.

Seufert, S. (2010): Gender-marketing: Kommunikationskonzept für die Einführung einer Produktionslinie für Singles. Diplomic Verlag GmbH, Hamburg.

Severin, A. (2005): Nachhaltigkeit als Herausforderung für das Kommunikationsmanagement in Unternehmen, in: Michelsen, G./Godemann, J. (Ed.)(2005): Handbuch Nachhaltigkeitskommunikation: Grundlagen und Praxis. Munich: Oekom Verlag, pp. 64 – 75.

Seyfang, G. (2001). Community Currencies: Small Change for a Green Economy, Environment and Planning A 33 (6), pp. 975-996.

SF (2011): Sustainability. URL [01.12.2011]: http://shambalafestival.org/festival-information/sustainability/.

SF (2012): Green To The Core. URL [06.03.2012]: http://www.shambalafestival.org/festival-information/sustainability/.

Shahd, M./Pols, A. (2010): Verbraucher informieren sich vor dem Kauf im Internet. Presseinformation 03.08.2010, Bitkom. Berlin.

Siebert, H. (2005): Nachhaltigkeitskommunikation: eine systemisch-konstruktivistische Perspektive, in: Michelsen, G./Godemann, J. (Ed.)(2005): Handbuch Nachhaltigkeitskommunikation: Grundlagen und Praxis. Munich: Oekom Verlag, pp. 132–140.

Slater, D. (1997). Consumer Culture & Modernity. Cambridge: Polity Press.

Small, K. & K. Van Dender (2005). The Effect of Improved Fuel Economy on Vehicles Miles Traveled: Estimating the Rebound Effect Using State Data, 1966-2001. UCEI Energy Policy and Economics, Working Paper 014, Berkeley: University of California Energy Institute.

Smith, A. (1776): An Inquiry into the Nature and Causes of the Wealth of Nations, Liberty Fund, Indianopolis.

Soper, K. (2007). Re-thinking the 'Good Life': The citizenship dimension of consumer dissatisfaction with consumption. Journal of Consumer Culture, 7(2), pp. 205-229.

Severin, A. (2005): Nachhaltigkeit als Herausforderung für das Kommunikationsmanagement in Unternehmen, in Michelsen, G./Godemann, J.(Ed.)(2005): Handbuch Nachhaltigkeitskommunikation, oekom Verlag, München, p. 64- 75.

Splore (2012): Trash Mountain. URL [05.02.2012]: http://splore.net/#/information/sustain.

Steedman, I. (2001). Consumption Takes Time: Implication for Economic Theory. London and New York: Routledge.

Steinkrauß, N./Gmelin, H./Günnel, S. (2008): Wettbewerbsanalyse In: Clement, M./Schusser, O./Papies, D. (2008): Ökonomie der Musikindustrie, 2nd edition, Wiesbaden, pp. 27-44.

Stiglitz, J. E. (2003): Globalization and Its Discontents, Columbia University, New York.

Stockrahm, S. (2011): Maßlosigkeit vergiftet unsere Lebensmittel. ZEIT ONLINE, 11.01.2011 - 16:12 Uhr, URL [25.11.2011]: http://www.zeit.de/wissen/umwelt/2011-01/dioxin-konsequenzen-bewusstsein.

Supersberger, N./Luhmann, H.-J. (2008): Die Endlichkeit von Erdöl und Erdgas, in Sachs (Ed.)(2008): Zukunftsfähiges Deutschland, 2008, 2nd Edition, Frankfurt am Main, pp. 41-51,

Thaler, R. H./Sunstein, C. R. (2009): nudge. Improving decisions about health wealth and happiness, Penguin Books, London.

Thielsch, M. T. (2008): Ästhetik von Websites. Wahrnehmung von Ästhetik und deren Beziehung zu Inhalt, Usability und Persönlichkeitsmerkmalen. MV Wissenschaft, Münster.

Thommen, J.-P./Achleitner, A.-K. (2006): Allgemeine Betriebswirtschaftslehre. Umfassende Einführung aus managementorientierter Sicht. 5th Edition, Gabler- Verlag, Wiesbaden.

Troendle, M. (2009): Von der Ausführungs- zur Aufführungskultur in Troendle, M. (Ed.)(2009): Das Konzert: neue Aufführungskonzepte für eine klassische Form, Bielefeld, pp. 21- 45.

UNEP (1992): Rio Declaration on Environment and Development, URL [05.02.2012]: http://www.unep.org/Documents.Multilingual/Default.asp?documentid=78&articleid=1163.

UNEP (2011): UNEP Goodwill Ambassadors Recognized For Putting Environment in the Spotlight. 25. 11.2011, Nairobi URL [07.12.2011]: http://www.unep.org/gwa/spotlight/doncheadleawards.asp).

Von Weizsäcker, E.U., A.B. Lovins & L.H. Lovins (1997). Factor Four: Doubling Wealth, Halving Resource Use. Earthscan, London.

van Parijs, P. (1991). Les deux écologismes, in F. De Roose et P.Van Parijs (eds.). La pensée écologiste. Bruxelles : De Boeck Université, pp.135-157.

ViVA CON AGUA (2012): Quellen der Freude. Resümee Scorpio-Festivals in 2011, URL [01.03.2012]: http://www.vivaconagua.org/index.htm?aktionen_festivals.

von Winterfeld, U. (2007): Keine Nachhaltigkeit ohne Suffizienz. Fünf Thesen und Folgerungen, Magazine Vorgänge, Magazine Nb. 3/2007, Humanistische Union, Berlin, pp. 46-54.

Warde, A. (1997): Consumption, Food & Taste. London, Thousand Oaks, New-Delhi: Sage Pub. Schumpeter 1920, Der österreichische Volkswirt.

Watzlawick, P. (1967): Some Tentative Axioms of Communication. In: Watzlawick, P./Beavin-Bavelas, J./Jackson, D. (1967): Pragmatics of Human Communication. A Study of Interactional Patterns. Pathologies and Paradoxes, Norton & Company, New York, pp. 48-71.

WaterAid (2011): Love your loo - caught on camera. URL [06.03.2012]: http://www.wateraid.org/uk/get_involved/events/festival_and_music_events/glastonbury/6760.asp.

Wehner, C. (1996): Überzeugungsstrategien in der Werbung. Eine Längsschnittanalyse von Zeitschriftenanzeigen des 20. Jhd. Opladen, Westdeutscher Verlag, Opladen.

Wehrspaun, M./Wehrspaun, C. (2005): Nachhaltigkeitskommunikation als politisches Instrument, in Michelsen, G./Godemann, J.(Ed.)(2005): Handbuch Nachhaltigkeitskommunikation, oekom Verlag, München, pp. 53- 63.

Weis, J. C. (2007): Kompakt Training Marketing, in: Olfert, K. (editor)(2007): Kompakt Training Praktische Betriebswirtschaft, 5th edition, HTWK Leipzig, Friedrich Kiehl Verlag, Ludwigshafen.

Weizsäcker, E. U. von/Lovins, A. B./Hunter, L. H. (1995): Faktor vier: Doppelter Wohlstand - halbierter Verbrauch: Doppelter Wohlstand - halbierter Verbrauch, Droemer Knaur, 6th edition, München.

Westbury, L. (2012): On the map: Greener Festival Award 2011 Winner, URL [20.02.2012]: http://www.agreenerfestival.com/2012/02/on-the-map-greener-festival-award-2011-winners/.

Wichmannn, J./Lucas, R. (2005): Innovationsfeld Event-Catering Wege zu einer nachhaltigen Ess- und Genusskultur – Projekt: Eventkultur und Nachhaltigkeit –, Wuppertal Institute.

Wirtz, B. W. (2007): Handbuch für Multichannel Marketing, DHV Speyer, Gabler Verlag, Wiesbaden.

Wöhe, G. (2005): Einführung in die Allgemeine Betriebswirtschaftslehre. 22th Edition, Verlag Franz Vahlen, Munich.

World Commission on Environment and Development (WCED)(1987): Our common future. Oxford: Oxford University Press.

Wünsch, U./Thuy, P. (2007): Handbuch Event- Kommunikation. Grundlagen und Best- Practice für erfolgreiche Veranstaltungen, Erich- Schmidt- Verlag, Berlin.

Xiang, L./Petrick, F. J.(2006): A Review of Festival and Event Motivation Studies, Event Management, Vol. 9, No. 4., pp. 239-245.

Zavestoski, S. (2001): Environmental Concern and Anti-consumerism in the Self-Concept. In: M. Cohen, and J. Murphy (Editors), Exploring Sustainable Consumption: Environmental Policy and the Social Sciences, Pergamon, pp.173-189.

Ziemann, A. (2007): Kommunikation der Nachhaltigkeit: Eine kommunikationstheoretische Fundierung, in: Michelsen, G./Godemann, J. (Ed.): Handbuch Nachhaltigkeitskommunikation: Grundlagen und Praxis, oekomVerlag, Munich, pp. 123 – 133.

Appendix

Appendix 1: Mail Openairguide.net

Von: "info@openairguide.net" <info@openairguide.net>
Gesendet: 02.02.2012 13:48:45
An: "Franziska Hillmer" <fhillmer@web.de>
Betreff: Re: Liste beliebter Festivals

Guten Tag Frau Hillmer,

Entschuldigung für die verspätete Antwort.

Die Beliebtheit der Festivals wird anhand der Seitenaufrufe ermittelt. Dabei werden die Klicks für ein Festival nur einmal pro Session gezählt. (d.h. ein User klickt 15 Bands an diesem Festival an, wird aber nur 1x in der Datenbank gezählt)

Die Datenbank, die diese Aufrufe zusammenzählt, ist seit ca. 2 Jahren in Betrieb. Ich denke, dass sich durch den Zeitraum der Erhebung durchaus abschätzen lässt, wie populär die Festivals sind. Es gilt allerdings zu beachten, dass die Mehrheit der Besucher meiner Website aus der Schweiz stammt, was sich z.B. in der deutlichen Spitzenposition des Southside Festivals zeigt.

Gerne überlasse ich Ihnen genauen Zugriffszahlen der aktuellen Top15-Festivals Deutschlands:
- Southside: 103'548
- Rock am Ring: 73'303
- Melt!: 67'832
- Rock im Park: 64'340
- Open Flair: 47'674
- Dockville: 39'689
- Hurricane: 37'621
- splash!: 36'711
- SonneMondSterne: 32'505
- Haldern Pop: 22'174
- Wacken: 22'022

- Highfield: 21'298
- Berlin Festival: 20'360
- Area4: 19'482
- Rock am See: 15'449

Falls Sie noch weitere Fragen haben, stehe ich Ihnen natürlich gerne zur Verfügung.

Freundliche Grüsse aus der Schweiz
Elio Bucher, openairguide.net

Appendix 2: The Winners of the Greener Festival Award 2011

The winners of the Greener Festival Award 2011 are:

Outstanding

Croissant Neuf Summer Party (England)
Falls Festival, Lorne, Victoria (Australia)
Falls Festival, Marion Bay, Tasmania (Australia)
Isle of Wight Festival (England)
Lightening in a Bottle (USA)
Oya Festival (Norway)
Peats Ridge (Australia)
Shambala (England)
Sunrise Celebration (England)
We Love Green (France)
Wood (England)
Woodford Festival (Australia)

Highly commended

Bestival (England)
Bonnaroo (USA)
Co-operative Cambridge Folk Festival (England)
Glastonbury Festival (England)
Grassroots (Jersey)
Lollapalooza (USA)
Malmo Festival (Sweden)
Island Vibe (Australia)
SOS 4:8 (Spain)

Commended

Austin City Limits (USA)
Calgary Folk Music Festival (Canada)
East Coast Bluesfest (Australia)
Festibelly (England)
Heineken Dia de la Musica (Spain)
Ilosaaririock (Finland)
Hadra Trance Festival (France)
The Open Air Festival (Czech Republic)
Rock for People (Czech Republic)
San Sebastian Festival (Spain)
Sonisphere (England)
Splendour Festival (England)

Splendour in the Grass (Australia)
Summer Sundae Weekender (England)
T-in-the-Park (Scotland)
Waveform (England)
Welcome to the Future (Netherlands)
WomAdelaide (Australia)

Improving

Camp Bestival (England)
Download (England)
Greenbelt Festival (England)
Hard Rock Calling (England)
Lounge on the Farm (England)
Radio 1 Big Weekend (England)
Wireless (England)

http://www.agreenerfestival.com/pdfs/AGFA_PRESS_RELEASE_2011.pdf

Appendix 3: Rock'n'Roll- Guide

Appendix 4: Facebook Festival Distribution of the Survey

Haldern Pop:

Rocken am Brocken:

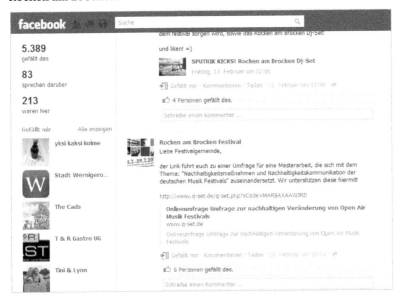

Southside:

Appendix: 5 Survey Results

Up From Space were only taken the German Results as the English Results (7 Participants) did not change the overall outcome.

Fragen kostet nichts. Q-Set.de

Umfrage zur nachhaltigen Veränderung von Open Air Musik Festivals

Seite 1: Dein Geschlecht

629 Teilnehmer

Weiblich	325
Männlich	304

Seite 1: Dein Alter

629 Teilnehmer

jünger als 18 Jahre	51
18 bis 24 Jahre	360
25 bis 29 Jahre	129
30 bis 39 Jahre	68
40 bis 49 Jahre	13
50 bis 59 Jahre	8
über 60	-

Seite 1: Deine derzeitige Tätigkeit

628 Teilnehmer

Schüler/in	124
Auszubildende/r	41
Student/in	270
Arbeitssuchend	11
Arbeitnehmer	160
Hausfrau/mann	1
Selbstständige/r	19
Rentner/in	2

Seite 1, Frage 1: Wie oft hast Du 2011...

628 Teilnehmer

	keinmal	1-mal	2-mal	3-mal	4-mal	5-mal	Mehr als 5-mal
...ein mehrtägiges Musik Festival besucht?	52	290	168	76	16	8	16
..eine Urlaubsreise unternommen (egal ob Kurztrip oder lange Reise)?	46	131	161	120	61	20	70

Seite 1, Frage 2: Wie oft willst Du 2012...

627 Teilnehmer

	keinmal	1-mal	2-mal	3-mal	4-mal	5-mal	Mehr als 5-mal
...ein mehrtägiges Musik Festival besuchen?	9	257	229	87	22	11	11
...eine Urlaubsreise unternehmen?	33	155	202	112	45	16	38

Seite 1, Frage 3: Welche/s Festival hast Du schon mal besucht?

625 Teilnehmer

Keins	16	
Haldern Pop	203	
Hurricane	114	
Melt!	53	
MS Dockville	18	
Open Flair	25	
Rock am Ring	114	
Rock im Park	89	
SonneMondSterne	22	
Southside	321	
Splash!	16	
Andere:	390	• Highfield (**14 x**) • Rock am See (**10 x**) • Taubertal (**10 x**) • Rocco del Schlacko (**8 x**) • Frequency (**6 x**) • Rocken am Brocken (**6 x**) • Chiemsee Reggae Summer (**4 x**) • Chiemsee Rocks (**4 x**) • summer breeze (**3 x**) • Sea of Love (**3 x**) • Area4 (**3 x**) • Area 4 (**3 x**)

...

Seite 1, Frage 4: Wie weit sind die von Dir bisher besuchten Musik Festivals jeweils von Deinem Wohnort entfernt? Nicht relevante Felder einfach frei lassen.

613 Teilnehmer

	bis 50 km	bis 250 km	bis 500 km	bis 800 km	über 800 km
Festival 1	177	281	126	23	4
Festival 2	79	229	120	24	6
Festival 3	58	113	72	32	8
Festival 4	32	62	30	17	8
Festival 5	22	36	12	8	10

Seite 1, Frage 5: Wie gestaltet sich Deine jährliche Urlaubs- & Festivalplanung?

622 Teilnehmer

Ich plane den Zeitraum der Reise/n so, dass ich mein/e Lieblingsfestival/s besuchen kann.	446
Ich fahre mit dem Auto in den Urlaub.	324
Ich fahre mit der Bahn in den Urlaub.	179
Ich unternehme eine private Flugreise pro Jahr.	181
Ich unternehme mehrere private Flugreisen pro Jahr.	62
Ohne die Festivals würde ich im Sommer wahrscheinlich eine zusätzliche Flugreise unternehmen.	96

Seite 1, Frage 6: Was ist Dir wichtiger?

631 Teilnehmer

	1	2	3	4	5	Durchschnitt
Urlaubsreise	39	156	230	164	42	3,02 (1907 / 631 Antworten)

Seite 1, Frage 7: Wie wichtig sind Dir die folgenden Aspekte für die Teilnahme an einem Festival?

	sehr wichtig	wichtig	weniger wichtig	unwichtig
Entspannte Atmosphäre	464	148	11	5
Kostenlose Parkplätze	178	195	180	68
Line Up (Liste der Musiker)	411	198	18	1
Neue Leute kennen lernen	81	217	285	43
Preiswertes Essen	59	229	290	46
Sauberkeit der sanitären Anlagen	278	255	81	14
Umweltschutzmaßnahmen der Veranstalter	122	302	165	37
Viel Zeit mit Freunden verbringen	428	167	23	2
Im Zelt schlafen	97	206	209	112

Seite 1, Frage 8: Das Festival "The Croissant Neuf Summer Party" hat ein umweltfreundliches Mitmachangebot zu seinem Markenzeichen gemacht - von Tanzworkshops bis zum Selberbauen von Windmühlen oder Holzarbeiten. Welche Rahmenprogrammpunkte fändest Du interessant?

631 Teilnehmer

	1	2	3	4	5	Durchschnitt
Bierbraukurs	103	184	112	74	158	3,00 (1893 / 631 Antworten)
Feuerwerk	53	172	118	115	173	3,29 (2076 / 631 Antworten)
Sportturnier (z. B. Fußball, Volleyball), wofür sich Teams anmelden können	97	207	101	101	125	2,92 (1843 / 631 Antworten)
Moto- Cross Show	27	79	80	116	329	4,02 (2534 / 631 Antworten)
Do it yourself- Workshops (z. B. Gemüseanbau in der Stadt, Brot backen)	64	153	109	125	180	3,32 (2097 / 631 Antworten)
Tanz- Workshop (z. B. Breakdance, Salsa)	59	117	98	143	214	3,53 (2229 / 631 Antworten)
Yoga –Workshop	62	110	94	113	252	3,61 (2276 / 631 Antworten)

Seite 1, Frage 9: Viele Festivals wollen mehr für Umwelt- und Klimaschutzmaßnahmen tun. Wie findest Du das?

629 Teilnehmer

sehr wichtig	267
wichtig	279
ist mir egal	44
nicht so wichtig	17
unwichtig	4
solche Maßnahmen bringen nichts	6
weiß nicht	12

Seite 2, Frage 10: Ticket- Kauf: Einige Festivals bieten die Zahlung eines Zusatzbetrages zur Kompensation der durchschnittlich durch den Teilnehmer verursachten CO_2- Emissionen an (ca. 2-5 €). Dieses Geld fließt in Klimaschutzprojekte, z. B. Aufforstungsmaßnahmen. Würdest Du Dich daran beteiligen?

611 Teilnehmer

Ja, eine gute Idee, um einen Beitrag zu leisten.	323
Ja, eine gute Idee, um das Gewissen zu beruhigen.	92
Unschlüssig	71
Nein, aber wenn ich mehr Geld verdienen würde, würde ich es tun.	84
Nein, dafür ist mir das Geld zu schade.	28
Weiß nicht	12

Seite 2, Frage 11: Durch die Anreise zum Festival entstehen viele Schadstoffemissionen. Einige Veranstalter bieten deshalb Bus-Shuttles und sogar Sonderzüge zum Festival an. Welche Vorzüge wären für Dich ausschlaggebend, um den Service zu nutzen?

603 Teilnehmer

	absolut	maßgeblich	eher nicht	absolut nicht

	maßgeblich	maßgeblich	maßgeblich	nicht maßgeblich
Ausstieg am Festival Haupteingang (statt Warten in der Autoschlange)	204	273	100	18
Kein eigener Fahrstress	163	245	143	49
Keiner deiner Freunde muss fahren	119	232	183	60
Neue Leute durch die Fahrt kennen lernen	49	168	276	103
Party vor der Party	62	177	239	116
Preisgünstiger als vergleichbare Fahrt mit eigenem Auto	203	253	102	41
Sicheres Ankommen	177	244	129	45
Umwelt und Klima schonen	129	304	130	27
Während des Festivals Shuttle-Service zum nächsten Supermarkt/Stadtzentrum	155	223	144	74
Zuverlässige Abfahrtszeiten und -orte	274	234	57	27

Seite 2:

103 Teilnehmer

Nichts davon überzeugt mich, ich reise lieber mit dem Auto an.	103

Seite 2, Frage 12: Musik- Festivals haben viele Sponsoringpartner. Sollten Sponsoren gewisse Nachhaltigkeitskriterien erfüllen?

625 Teilnehmer

Ja, Unternehmen als Sponsoren auswählen, die sich überzeugend für Umwelt- und Klimaschutz einsetzen.	301
Das ist mir egal.	161
Nein, ich finde das übertrieben.	104
Weiß nicht	59

Seite 2, Frage 13: Während des Festivals wird viel verkauft, egal ob Lebensmittel oder Klamotten. Wie ist Deine Meinung zu folgenden Aussagen?

627 Teilnehmer

	Ich stimme zu	Ist mir nicht so wichtig	Ist mir egal	Ich stimme nicht zu	Weiß nicht
Lebensmittel sollten nach Möglichkeit aus der Region des Festivalstandortes stammen.	300	181	112	29	5
Lebensmittel sollten nach Möglichkeit aus biologischem Anbau sein.	164	209	169	76	7
Lebensmittel aus anderen Ländern sollten fair gehandelt sein, d. h. dass den Erzeugern ein angemessener Mindestpreis garantiert wird.	383	151	65	14	9
Festivals sollten mehr vegetarische Gerichte anbieten.	198	122	208	90	8
Festivals sollten mehr vegane Gerichte anbieten.	74	109	258	167	15
Angebotene Kleidung sollte aus Bio-Baumwolle hergestellt sein.	71	159	234	142	18
Angebotene Kleidung sollte aus fair gehandelter Baumwolle sein.	238	167	156	44	15

Seite 2, Frage 14: Auf dem "Glastonbury"- Festivalgelände gibt es einen Ort, wo es um

130

konkrete Wege zu einem nachhaltigen Lebensstil geht. Unter Mithilfe von Umweltorganisationen können Besucher bspw. testen, wie mit einem Fahrrad Batterien aufgeladen werden, sich an Diskussionen beteiligen, lernen in der Großstadt zu gärtnern und dort auftretenden Bands zuhören. Wie ist Deine Meinung dazu?

627 Teilnehmer

Sehr interessant, ich würde garantiert hingehen.	68	
Interessant, ich würde wahrscheinlich hingehen.	257	
Ich habe kein Interesse, mich auf dem Festival mit Klima- und Umweltschutz zu beschäftigen.	262	
Ich habe generell kein Interesse mich mit Klima- und Umweltschutz zu beschäftigen.	7	
Andere Antwort/Kommentar:	33	• interessant, für mich nicht so relevant • würds mal anschaun • ich würde wahrscheinlich hingehen, sofern keine (für mich interessante) band einen auftritt hat.

Seite 2, Frage 15: Um den Plastik-Müll zu reduzieren, bietet das 'Lightning in a Bottle Festival' gratis frisches Wasser an und animiert die Besucher dazu, ihre eigene Flasche und sogar Geschirr mitzubringen, welches beim Kauf der Lebensmittel verwendet werden kann. Wie beurteilst Du das?

620 Teilnehmer

Super, ich bin dabei.	326
Es ist okay, da es der Sache dient.	235
Ist mir egal.	21
Ich finde das nicht so toll, aber immerhin gibt es Wasser gratis.	20
Übertrieben, was soll ich noch alles mitschleppen?	18

Seite 2:

12 Teilnehmer

Andere Antwort/Kommentar:	11	• Ich nehme nur eigenes Geschirr und eigenes Essen mit. Für Wasser einen auffüllbaren Kanister! • Sollte es überall geben. • Grundsätzlich eine sehr gute Idee, nur die Umsetzung stelle ich mir für Festivalbesucher etwas nervig vor. • Es wär super, wenn man seine Wasserflasche mit reinnehmen dürfte und die immer wieder voll machen könnte.

Seite 2, Frage 16: Das "Rothbury"- Festival verwendet kompostierbares Plastikgeschirr. Damit der Müll richtig getrennt und entsorgt werden kann, kontrolliert ein Team, erkennbar an T-Shirts mit 'One person who cares'- Aufschrift, dass Mülleimer genutzt werden und assistiert bei Bedarf beim Wegwerfen. Welcher Aussage stimmst Du zu?

623 Teilnehmer

Ich finde solche Teams sinnvoll.	337	
Sie helfen den Müll auf dem Gelände zu reduzieren.	448	
Sie haben Vorbildcharakter für das eigene Umweltbewusstsein.	285	
Ist mir egal.	40	
Ich würde mich durch die Teams eingeschränkt fühlen.	48	
Um den Müll sollte sich nach dem Festival gekümmert werden- nicht währenddessen.	29	
Andere Antwort/Kommentar:	25	• das klingt fast zu deutsch! • sie sollten dazu beitragen, dass am ende des festivals jeder seinen müll gerecht entsorgt • Kommt drauf an ob sich diese Leute als Oberlehrermüllpolizei aufführen oder wirklich freundlich sind und einfach helfen. • ...sie dürfen nicht zu sehr nerven :D

Seite 2, Frage 17: Die Kampagne ‚Love your tent' des "Isle of Wight"- Festivals soll Teilnehmer anregen, ihre Campingsachen wieder mitzunehmen. Die Veranstalter sagen, dass es 485 Arbeitsstunden braucht, um Zelte etc. zu entfernen und dass die Maßnahmen viel Geld kosten, welches sonst zur Unterhaltung genutzt werden könnte. Wie stehst Du zu den folgenden Aussagen?

631 Teilnehmer

	1	2	3	4	5	Durchschnitt
Ich staune, dass so viele Leute ihre Zelte liegen lassen.	388	155	32	30	26	1,65 (1044 / 631 Antworten)
Mich ärgert, dass so viele Leute ihre Zelte liegen lassen.	241	205	123	42	20	2,04 (1288 / 631 Antworten)
Wahrscheinlich werde ich in Zukunft darauf achten, dass Freunde keine Zelte liegen lassen.	169	215	163	56	28	2,30 (1452 / 631 Antworten)
Ich stelle fest, dass ich mir darüber noch keine Gedanken gemacht habe.	78	76	111	120	246	3,60 (2273 / 631 Antworten)

Seite 2, Frage 18: Die Preisfrage: Auf Veranstaltungen sind die Preise meistens höher. Trotzdem ist zertifiziertes Biofleisch üblicherweise noch teurer als konventionelles Fleisch. Bei welcher Botschaft würdest Du zugreifen?

622 Teilnehmer

Knackige Bratwurst für 2,50 €	308
Knackige Bio- Bratwurst für 3,00 €	214

Bin Vegetarier	93
Bin Veganer	7

Appendix 6: Comments Q. 7 – General Ambitions

Alcohol: "Bier", "saufen", "Alkohol", "Bier- sehr wichig", "Freibier", "saufen!", "Bier ;-)", Bier trinken

Surrounding: Möglichkeit Schwimmen zu gehn, am besten einen See, Alltagsalternative, Neue Bands entdecken, Sex!, Flanky Ball!, Party nach den Bands, angebotene Aktivitäten neben der Musik: shoppen, Kunst, Party

Feeling: "Stimmung genießen, Spaß haben, das ganze Feeling, einfach geil!", "Keine Mallorca-Kultur", "freiheit im sein, aussehen, etc", "das es kein zu großes Festival ist",

Music: musik genießen, "neue Bands entdecken" (2x)

Organization: "gute Organisation", "Gratis Kondome", "Eine gute Zeiteinteilung/ - organisation", "gute Informationen vom Veranstalter über das Festival", Festivalorganisation beim Einlass: sehr wichtig! auf dem Deichbrand war das furchtbar

Ticket: "Kosten für das Ticket"/"Ticketpreis", Preiswertes Ticket, Ticketpreis

Gelände: "sauberes Festivalgelände" (2x), "Erlaubnis von Glas-Flaschen", "Befestigte Wege zum Festivalgelände!", Kurze Wege auf dem Festivalgelände, Zeltplatzbeleuchtung

Accommodation: "wohnwagen platz", "Wohnmobil camping plätze", Wohnmobil-Stellplätze "Unterkunft, wenn möglich kein Zelt. (Pension Rolling Stone Weekender, OF und RAB)", sehr wichtig: NICHT im Zelt schlafen"

Security: Sicherheit Gewaltfrei und keine KrimInalität/ friedliches Beisammensein (keine Gewalt oder Kriminalität)/ "Security-Politik"/ dazu friedliches Beisamensein, genügend Security, Wichtig ist Sicherheit zwar, es nervt ständig kontrolliert, Ausreichend Sicherheit durch Security, Polizei und vorallem Erste-Hilfe Sanitäter!zu werden.

Distance: Entfernung, Entfernung zum Wohnort

Umwelt: Umweltmaßnahmen: bisher keine Gedanken zu gemacht. Finde aber gut, dass ein wichtiger Bestandteil des Festival, die Natur, durch dieses nicht geschädigt wird

Wishes: Alkoholische Getränke mit aufs Bühnengelände bringen dürfen, ausreichende Trinkwasserversorgung; Bereitstellung von Regencapes bei schlechtem Wetter

Diverses: wir sind wohnmobiler :), Bulli

Weather: Gutes Wetter, Regen versaut einem oft das schönste Festival. Bei manchen Festivals habe ich fast keine Lust mehr hinzugehen, weil es jedes Mal regnet

Appendix 7: General Comments Structured

Comments

83

		13,2%
Suggestions for festival operators	Why not involve the artists and musicians in the sustainable festival concept. Many of them already have an interest in this and they could help to make a "hot" topic out of it.	**Bands**
	.. sollte man sich vielleicht auch konkret an die Bands richten und versuchen Strom zu sparen oder einen Teil selbst zu erzeugen (bei den meisten Festivals ist ja gutes Wetter)	
	Auf vielen Festivals werden Tetrapak-Behälter zugelassen, Mehrwegflaschen nicht. Beides ist umweltschädlich, deshalb sollte auf die am wenigsten umweltschädliche Variante zurückgegriffen werden. Fairere Preise für Essen sollten eingeführt werden, damit nicht so viel Dosenessen im Vorfeld gekauft werden muss usw - und wichtig: Bio heißt nicht = besser! Regionale Produkte die nicht im Bioverfahren hergestellt werden müssen nicht unbeding schlechter sein, so meine Meinung. Spätestens wenn Bioprodukte aus dem Ausland angeschafft werden müssen, erübrigt sich der Sinn von Bioprodukten, siehe Aldi- oder Lidl-Bioprodukte.	**Food**
	Leider kommt für mich, auf Grund der Preise auf dem Festival nicht in Frage, alle Lebensmittel und Getränke dort zu kaufen. Und so bleibt mir nur der Transport mit dem Auto.	
	GENERELL BILLIGERE GETRÄNKE UND SPEIßEN ANBIETEN!	
	solange es kein einheitliches bio-siegel gibt, bin ich da eher kritisch. zumal die grundlagen für zertifikate zu unterschiedlich sind und bio-produkte meiner meinung nach ihren anspruch auf ein solches siegel verlieren, wenn sie erst hunderte von kilometern durch die weltgeschichte gefahren werden. wenn man wirklich auf nachhaltigkeit bedacht ist und so viel wert auf bio-lebensmittel legt, dann sollte man auch so konsequent sein und bei lokalen erzeugern kaufen. und dann vielleicht auch die finger von orts-/jahreszeitfremden lebensmitteln lassen.	
	Backfisch	
	Ich bringe mein Essen selbst mit, daher kaufe ich eigentlich nie auf Festivals Nahrungsmittel.	
	Vorallem veganes Essen	
	Reise mit Kind (geht nicht zu jedem Festival), da ist Anreise kein Thema, Versorgung mit vernünftigem Essen schon.	
	Ich kaufe nicht selten Essen auf Festivals	
	Viel erschreckender als liegengebliebene Zelte finde ich die Unmengen an Lebensmitteln, die auf Festivals übrig bleiben. Z.B. ungeöffnete Dosen Ravioli, noch originalverpacktes Brot etc.	
	aber nur wenn auch Bio drin ist. Die Gefahr des Missbrauchs ist gross.	
	alle anstrengungen von festivals bzgl. einer vermehrten nachhaltigkeit sollten unabdingbar verknüpft werden mit propagierter transparenz. insbesondere festivals wie "haldern", die eh immer ausverkauft sind und eine klientel anziehen, die dem gedanken (das unterstell ich jetzt einfach mal) sehr offen und positiv gegenüberstehen, hätten die möglichkeit, den gedanken des "korrekten" zusammenkommens in ihr profil zu übernehmen.	**Communication**
	Auf dem Summer Breeze Festival gibt es **Anreize**, nämlich großformatige **Poster des Festivalgeländes** aus der Vogelperspektive, wenn man **am letzten Tag mindestens 3 Säcke Müll abgibt**. Vielleicht ist das eine gute Methode. Ich hab's jedenfalls bisher jedes Jahr getan. ;)	
	In Roskilde gibt es ein sehr gutes Pfandsystem für Flaschen, Dosen etc. Das animiert viele zum sammeln und Müll reduzieren!	**WASTE**
	Sinnvoll fände ich es, wenn nach Festivalende **Müll und Pfandflaschen vor Ort abgegeben** werden könnten, Müllbeutel z.B. im Tausch für einen Becher Kaffee. **Vielen Besuchern**, vor allem denen ohne Auto, **ist es vermutlich zu viel, das alles wieder mitzuschleppen.**	
	Bei Rock am Ring/Park und South Side sollten die **Zeiten für die Rückgabe voller Mülltüten deutlich erweitert** werden, dann würde ich auch so mal übers Gelände laufen und Müll einsammeln!	
	[Zugegeben wird auf Festival vieles übertrieben. Die perfekte Sauberkeit aber gehört viel mehr in natürliche Umgebung (z.B. beim Bergleben mal jeder allen Müll wieder mit hinunterzunehmen!) Auf Festivals mal nen Becher / Flasche / Serviette fallenzulassen ist angesichts der herrschenden Grundstimmung und des meist geschlossenen Geländes vertretbar. Es sollte seitens der Behörden darauf geachtet werden, dass Veranstalter den Veranstaltungsort nach der Veranstaltung pico bello "zurückgeben".]	

Ich war die letzten 2 Jahre auf dem Southside Festival. Durch den Schlamm war den Leuten das Abfallverständnis völlig abhanden, viele haben extrem viel zurück gelassen. Das finde ich sehr falsch. Der **Müllpfand müsste deutlich angehoben werden** (20€ min) und **nicht nur 1 Müllsack pro Person**. Bzw sollte das gesamte Müllkonzept überdacht werden. Außerdem war beides Mal die Stimmung am Sonntag Abend einfach nur noch "ZERSTÖREN" und "ANARCHIE". Da muss sich was ändern, das ist so echt unschön.

Meiner Meinung nach sollte auf Festivals die Musik im Vordergrund sein und nicht die Workshops, jedoch sollte man schon auf Mülltrennung und so achten, ich glaube, dass so Sachen die "vorgegeben" werden, eher eingehalten werden, als andere.

finde es schlimm, wie wenig es die Menschen kümmert, dass sie das Festivalgelände schon nach einem Tag **wie eine Müllhalde** aussieht, da **vergeht einem teilweise die Lust aufs Festival und fühlt sich eher unwohl**. Es ist auch erschreckend, wieviel Müll sich in so kurzer Zeit ansammelt. Ein Festival à la Woodstock stelle ich mir so nicht vor.

Es gibt immer **zu wenig Mülleimer** und diese sind immer überfüllt. Von Mülltrennung ganz zu schweigen.

Man kann auf Festivals etwas umweltbewusst vorgehen und den Aufräumern Arbeit ersparen. Aber bei jeder Kleinigkeit darauf zu achten, nervt einfach und ist meist nicht gut für die Zeltgemeinschaft. Außer man reist nur mit Ökos. Ansonsten kann sowas echt sinnvoll sein, ich finde vor allem große Aktionen wie viva con aqua auf dem Southside brignen wirklich was ;) **Letztes Jahr sind die zum ersten mal mit einem riesen Wagen überden Campingplatz gefahren und haben die Leute aufgefordert den Müll draufzuwerfen. Das macht dann sogar Spass, denn es wurde ne richtige Karawane von Leuten+Typ mit Megafon und Mukke auf dem Wagen. TOP!**

Ich bin immer wieder total erstaunt, was die Jugendlichen alles liegen lassen: Zelte, Schlafsäcke etc, die müssen einfach zu viel Geld haben!

Der Müll auf den normalen Zeltplätzen hat enorm zugenommen die vergangenen Jahre. Ein Grund für mich/uns **Zelten** so weit wie möglich **zu vermeiden und in WoMo bzw. Pension/Hotel zu übernachten.** Bsp. **Hurricane ist unerträglich geworden,** nur Müll und Chaos ab dem ersten Tag auf den Zeltplätzen.]

Gute Ansatzpunkte (Bsp. eigenes Geschirr oder kompostierbares Geschirr),

Die beste Nachhaltigkeitsaktivität: Nach dem Festival über den Zeltplatz schlendern und nach geeigneter liegengebliebener Campingausrüstung "shoppen"

zum Thema Zelt: beim Roskilde Festival werden **zurückgebliebene Zelte an die Obdachlosenhilfe gespendet**, kann also auch was Gutes haben..

Tickets sollten eine Option auf Anfahrt mit der Bahn zu vegünstigten Konditionen bekommen	Travel
Die Anreise per Shuttlebus kommt für mich wegen des vielen Gepäcks nicht in Frage	
Ich werde wahrscheinlich auch in Zukunft mit dem Auto zum Festival reisen, weil es einfach viel zu aufwendig ist sein ganzes Gepäck und vor allem die Lebensmittel udn Getränke mit Zug und Bus zum Festiva. zu transportieren. Darüber sollten sich die Veranstalter mal Gedanken machen. Ich wäre gerne bereit für eine Unterstützung beim Transport etwas extra zu zahlen.	
Die meißten Fragen treffen auf mich nicht so zu, da meine ganzen leute und ich mit dem caravan(alte vw busse)auf festivals fahren.dadurch ergeben sich bei uns die ein oder anderen probleme wie zelte dalassen oder mit dem zug fahren nicht.bei finde ich es dann schade,dass es für caravans extra kostenpflichtige tickets gibt obwohl bei uns tendentiell weniger umweltbelastung und müllbeseitigung erforderlich ist(meiner meinung nach)	
Vergleichbar zum Glastonbury kann man auf dem Melt! durch Fahrradfahren seinen Handyakku aufladen. Das Festival hat auch irgendeinen Greenaward bekommen, wenn ich richtig informiert bin. Ansonsten wünsch ich Dir viel Erfolg bei deiner Masterarbeit! Ich find es ist ein super Thema und ich hoffe, dass dir genug Musikliebhaber und Naturfreunde gewissenhaft antworten werden :)	Service
wenn seen in der nähe sind (haldern pop) abbaubares shampoo und abbaubare seife anbieten	
Why not involve the artists and musicians in the sustainable festival concept. Many of them already have an interest in this and they could help to make a "hot" topic out of it.	
Möglichkeit mind. 1-2 Liter Wasser ins Gelände mitnehmen zu können / Viele kostenlose Wasserspender / Discounter auf dem Gelände (Greenfield 2011)	
wenn seen in der nähe sind (haldern pop) abbaubares shampoo und abbaubare seife anbieten	

135

Green Camping auf dem Southside ist ne **gute Sache** in diese Richtung!	**Green Camping**
Greencamping bei Southside war ein Schritt in die richtige Richtung	
Ich finde das Grren Camping auf dem Southside Fesival schon einen guten Ansatz und habe dies **auch genutzt**	
Grün Zelten!	
Green Camping **sollte weiterentwickelt werden**. Hier könnte der Zwang bestehen, alles wieder so zu hinterlassen wie man es vorgefunden hat. Im Gegenzug sind die Camping Tickets leicht vergünstigt. [Der Müll auf den normalen Zeltplätzen hat enorm zugenommen die vergangenen Jahre. Ein Grund für mich/uns Zelten so weit wie möglich zu vermeiden und in WoMo bzw. Pension/Hotel zu übernachten. Bsp. Hurricane ist unerträglich geworden, nur Müll und Chaos ab dem ersten Tag auf den Zeltplätzen.]	
Aktionen wie das Green-Camping auf dem Southside oder dem Hurricane im letzten Jahr finde ich sehr wichtig und **unterstützenswert.** Toll, wenn dieser Bereich dann auch **noch näher am Bühnenbereich** ist und dort vor allem **entspannte Menschen zelten - und keine, die am Festivaleingang ihre Sozialisierung u. gesunden Menschenverstand abgeben.**	
Sehr schwer einige Fragen zu beantworten..Einerseits ist es natürlich sehr vorbildlich, wenn auch Festivals sich an gewisse klimaschützende Maßnahmen halten würden..**Jedoch gehört Müll und das Zelte-verbrennen am Ende eines Festivals irgendwie dazu.** Und die bisherigen Bemühungen **(zB Green Camps) waren einfach nur schlecht organisiert und haben gestört.** Festivalzeit ist **Gammelzeit.** 3 Tage lang nicht duschen und Alk konsumieren ;) Ich glaube viele Besucher würden schon aus Prinzip gewisse Vorgaben (zB Mülltrennung/sofortige Entsorgung) nicht einhalten. Bzw zu faul/betrunken sein :D	
Green-Camping ist ein super Angebot, was wir auch auf dem Hurricane bereits genutzt haben. Dort wurde z.B. darauf geachtet, dass der Müll nicht einfach auf den Boden geschmissen wird.	
Green camping vom southside finde ich sinnvoll.....wer will kann ohne Müll leben, wer die sau rauslassen will kann trotzdem in anarchie leben	
Festivals sind halt so ne Sache.. Klar ist es wichtig sich um Klimaschutz und Umwelt Gedanken zu machen, aber das Festivalfeeling sollte dadurch trotzdem nicht eingeschränkt werden. Vlt kann man ja so etwas wie günstigere Tickets gegen Verpflichtung danach beim Aufräumen oder ähnlichem zu helfen einführen.. K.A..	**Tickets**
Ich finde es schade,dass die Leute Festivals brauchen,damit sie es verstehen und man es ihnen eintrichtern kann. Es sollte von alleine kommen. Deswegen an alles Festivals die es tun - Hut ab!	
Grundsätzlich finde ich die ganze An- bzw. Abreisefrage problematisch...da man mit den umweltfreundlicheren Verkehrsmitteln komplett unflexibel ist und man gerade das Auto braucht, da doch meistens mehr dabei ist als alle Personen tragen können. Wir versuchen es immer so zu regel, dass wir ein Auto+ Anhänger voll packen..die 4 stärksten Jungs damit fahren und der Rest falls ein Bundeslandticket vorhanden ist, dieses auch benutzt! Man sollte evtl. vergünstigte Fahrkarten von Wohnortbahnhof zum Festival anbieten, damit noch mehr Leute diese Möglichkeit in Betracht ziehen. Meiner Meinung nach ist gerade die Anreise der Punkt an dem man als erstes Ansetzen sollte, wenn es um Umweltschutz geht, da es aufgrund des genannten Beispiels der vergünstigten Fahrkarten für Festivalkartenkäufer vom Wohnort zum Festival, dieses Problem in die Hand zu nehmen!!!!!!!!!!	
Die Festival-Tickets sind allgemein zu teuer.	
wenns nur 3 euro wären^^ [*remark for CO2- compensatinon*]	
Ich studiere selbst Umweltmanagament am Umwelt Campus Birkenfeld und interessiere mich sehr für diese Fragestellungen. Allerdings will man auf einem Festival auch einfach eine Sau sein dürfen.. Vlt sollte man den Besuchern einfach keine Wahl geben sondern einfach strickter durchgreifen. Cool, dass ihr euch mit dem Thema befasst!	**Generally**
Vorallem veganes Essen, bessere Muelltrennung und effiziente Sanitaere Anlagen halte ich fuer sehr wichtig und lohnend um ein Festival umweltfreundlich zu betreiben!	
Sehr schwer einige Fragen zu beantworten..Einerseits ist es natürlich sehr vorbildlich, wenn auch Festivals sich an gewisse klimaschützende Maßnahmen halten würden..Jedoch gehört Müll und das Zelte-verbrennen am Ende eines Festivals irgendwie dazu. [Und die bisherigen Bemühungen (zB Green Camps) waren einfach nur schlecht organisiert und haben gestört.] Festivalzeit ist Gammelzeit. 3 Tage lang nicht duschen und Alk konsumieren ;) Ich glaube viele Besucher würden schon aus Prinzip gewisse Vorgaben (zB Mülltrennung/sofortige Entsorgung) nicht einhalten. Bzw zu faul/betrunken sein :D	

Der feiernde Mensch und Festivalbesucher ist im Regelfall bei solchen Veranstaltungen um sich zu amüsieren. "Probleme" jeglicher Art werden dann ausgeblendet. Da werden ja selbst, die sonst großgeschriebenen, Hygienemaßnahmen missachtet, nach dem Motto "einmal im Jahr..". Von daher finde ich es sehr sinnvoll, ja sogar erforderlich, dass Maßnahmen von den Festival-Betreibern eingeleitet werden.

Umweltschutz und nachhaltiges Verhalten sind auf einem Festival wichtig, man sollte die Besucher, für die ein Festival evtl. wie ein Urlaub ist, jedoch nicht ständig damit konfrontieren, sondern ihnen die einfach die Möglichkeit bieten, sich darüber zu informieren, wenn sie möchten, sie nur bei Fehlverhalten ansprechen.

Zu den Sponsoren: Ich würde mir eine Antwort wünschen, welcher eine langfristige Planung "nachhaltigkeitsgerechter" Sponsoren gerecht wird. Eine schnelle Änderung wird nicht möglich sein, wenn denn. Zusätzlich würde ich immer zum Handbrot oder zu Nudeln greifen, da ich zwar Fleisch esse, jedoch nicht gerne. Also das lieber das frischgemachte Handbrot für 4 Euro. :) Und ein kleiner Hinweis zur Anreise, der ausschlaggebende Punkt für die Autoanreise wird wohl das Gepäck bei vielen sein. Dazu fehlt eine Frage. :(

Wie schon erwähnt, ist die Musik bei Festivals zunächst einmal das Wichtigste. Trotzdem ist es eine gute Sache, dass auf Mülltrennung bzw. allgemeine Müllreduzierung geachtete wird. Allerdings gehen Gemüseanbau oder Windrädchen-Bauanleitungen doch ein bisschen zu weit und sind für mich gänzlich uninteressant und fehl am Platz.

Festivals sind ein Großereigniss, ich gehe hin wegen den tollen Bands. Alles was mit umweldfreundlichkeit bei Festivals zu tuhen hat, unterstütze ich!

Schön, dass sich darüber Gedanken gemacht werden!

Da die Tickets i.d.R. eh sehr teur sind, kann man meiner Meinung nach auch noch ein paar Euro für die Nachhaltigkeit und den Umweltschutz drauf legen. Darauf kommt es bei dem eh schon hohen Preis auch nicht mehr an. Wer 3€ und mehr für ein Bier auf dem Gelände ausgeben kann, sollte auch etwas für nachfolgende Festivalgänger investieren, damit sie ebenfalls viel Spaß in der hoffentlich noch intakten Natur) haben. Hoffentlich werden die gesparten Müllensorgungskosten auch von den Eintrittskarten abgezogen. PS: sehr schönes Thema für eine Masterarbeit :)

Gute Ansatzpunkte (Bsp. eigenes Geschirr oder kompostierbares Geschirr),jedoch sollte man sich vielleicht auch konkret an die Bands richten und versuchen Strom zu sparen oder einen Teil selbst zu erzeugen (bei den meisten Festivals ist ja gutes Wetter)

Während eines Festivals mache ich mir wenig gedanken über Umweltschutz. Übertriebenes Umweltbewusstsein finde ich häufig sehr anstrengend. Aus diesem Grund möchte ich zumindest bei Festivals davon verschont bleiben. Werden jedoch Ideen umgesetzt, die ich"beiläufig" nutzen kann, so finde ich das durchaus gut!

Ich bin so schon sehr für die Umwelt und Nachhaltigkeit engagiert, auf einem Festival darf es deshalb dann auch mal ein Dosen Bier oder andere Umweltschädliche Sachen geben - Aber kein Fleisch :D

Umweltschutz ist wichtig, sollte aber nicht mit der Peitsche umgesetzt werden. Auch ist der Umweltschutz der Veranstalter doch häufig völlig schwachsinnig; überall auf Müllvermeidung machen und dann umweltfreundliche Glasflaschen verbieten

Grundsätzlich gehe ich wg Musik auf Festivals, ich hab keinen Bock irgendeiner verstrahlten Tussis erklären zu müssen, daß ich keinen Bock darauf habe, meinen Namen zu tanzen. Ich habe meinen Müll immer korrekt entsorgt & finde es auch wichtig, daß man gewisse umweltstandards einhält. Man kann aber auch alles übertreiben, ich hab keinen Bock auf ökofaschisten.

ich bin mir nicht sicher,ob die masse der meist jugendlichen konsumenten schon ein umweltbewußtsein entwickelt hat und überhaupt interesse an diesem fragebogen hat. den meisten geht es irgendwie um party und betäubung-was an sich noch nicht verwerflich ist. aber die mondlandschaft und die müllberge, die während des festivals entstehen, stoßen mich als alten sack schon auch ab.es kostet immer überwindung, sich solch einem "abenteuer" doch noch einmal zu stellen.zu stellen

Mich wunderts wirklich, dass Festivals wie das Southside jedes Jahr wieder stattfinden, da ich mir nicht vorstellen kann, dass die Southside Crew die Location tatsächlich innerhalb eines Jahres wieder sauber bringt :D Um ehrlich zu sein war ich schon leicht geschockt von den Bergen von Müll, die letztes Jahr übrig geblieben sind, aber auch von der Mentalität vieler Festivalbesucher, die scheinbar mit Absicht (Dosenraviolie in die Luft jagen) Müll produzieren und selbigen bewusst liegen lassen. Alles in allem bin ich durchaus bereit mehr Geld für die Tickets zu bezahlen, wenn der Ertrag sinnvoll in viele der oben genannten Maßnahmen/Möglichkeiten investiert wird.

	Ich arbeite selbst auf einem Festival, ich denke, dass Besucher hauptsächlich auf den Spaß aus sind und sich auf einem Festival eher weniger für Umweltschutz interessieren. Der Spaßfaktor steht im Vordergrund.
	Bei Großveranstaltungen wie Festivals sollte die Musik im Vordergrund stehen und nicht aus welchen Materialien das T-shirt ist das ich kaufe. Das ist mir an so einem Ort doch vollkommen egal. Dort bin ich um Spaß zu haben und den Alltag zu vergessen und mich nicht um die alltäglichen Belange zu kümmern. Sollte es wirklich zu Änderungen kommen, wie etwa bessere Mülltrennung, Aufsichtspersonen wie oben genannt, dann muss das nicht ich bestimmen sondern der Veranstalter!
	Wenn man an "Festival" denkt, steht der Gedanke der Nachhaltigkeit und das Umweltbewusstsein im Hintergrund. Ich denke, dass ist aus der "Festival-Tradition" entstanden und daher, dass Festivals ein Ort und eine Zeit sind, in der man sich komplett gehen lässt. Die Leute (auch die, die sonst umweltbewusster sind) auf ein umweltbewussten Umgang auf Festivals zu bewegen, wird viele Schrite und viel Zeit brauchen.
	Die Ideen sind super auch mit den Workshops aber ich denke es ist schwer umsetzbar da der Großteil bei Festivals nur an Party und Alkohol denkt..
	Sehr schwer einige Fragen zu beantworten..Einerseits ist es natürlich sehr vorbildlich, wenn auch Festivals sich an gewisse klimaschützende Maßnahmen halten würden..Jedoch gehört Müll und das Zelte-verbrennen am Ende eines Festivals irgendwie dazu. Und die bisherigen Bemühungen (zB Green Camps) waren einfach nur schlecht organisiert und haben gestört. Festivalzeit ist Gammelzeit. 3 Tage lang nicht duschen und Alk konsumieren ;) Ich glaube viele Besucher würden schon aus Prinzip gewisse Vorgaben (zB Mülltrennung/sofortige Entsorgung) nicht einhalten. Bzw zu faul/betrunken sein :D
Remakrs for a Sustainable Development	SuperThema - hier gibt es ganz viel zu tun! Spaß und Nachhaltigkeit schließen sich aus meiner Sicht nicht aus
	Schonmal dran gedacht, dass es eben nicht nur bio und das Gegenteil dazu die schädliche Massentierzucht mit vielen Pestiziden ect. gibt, sondern eben auch noch eine nicht-bio Landwirtschaft, die aber kaum schädlicher als bio ist?
	Ich halte mich zwar für Umweltbewust, stehe aber überhaupt nicht auf diesen Bio"wahn", wie man anhand meiner Antworten wohl bemerkt. Das hat aber nichts mit den Preisen zu tun, um die Gründe genau zu erklären, ist hier allerdings nicht genug Platz. Aber ich finde jedenfalls nicht, dass sich das widerspricht. ;-)
	was auf der Phäno - Ebene nach wie vor ein Problem darstellt: die Möglichkeit zu nachhaltigem, klimaschützenden Verhalten ist vor allem eine Frage des Einkommensbereiches und der jeweiligen Bildungsnähe, dürfte aber in diesem Sinne kein "Luxus" sein!
	Bio und Umweltschutz ist nicht immer das Selbde. Auch wenn man kein Bio-Fan ist, kann man Umweltschutz für wichtig erachten.
Remarks to the Survey	Der Fragebogen ist leider etwas durchschaubar und du solltest bei der Auswertung den Faktor "soziale Erwünschtheit" berücksichtigen. Bzw. (etwas unwissenschaftlicher): "sich selber belügen und besser darstellen, als man eigentlich ist"
	Is ja alles schön und gut!
	ich mag keine Bratwurst :)
	Frage 18: würde nicht zugreifen aber bin kein Vegetarier oO
	Ich bin an den Ergebnissen interessiert. Kontakt: fastolph_gamwich@web.de
	Gute Ansprechpartner: http://www.greenmusicinitiative.de/
	Manche fragen sind irgendwie leicht suggestiv bzw. haben bei 4 tatsächlichen nud 2 wirkliche Antwortmöglichkeiten (e.g. Fr. 12)
	Viel Erfolg bei der Masterarbeit!
	Viel Erfolg bei deiner Arbeit!
	nettes thema für ne masterarbeit ;)
	Werbefreier Fragebogen wäre besser... sonst spannendes Thema! Viel Erfolg!
	gutes Ding mit der Masterarbeit zu dem Thema. Ich hoffe du kannst damit was bewirken, damit das Müllproblem bei Festivals verbessert wird. Grüße aus Stuttgart
	Viel Glück!!

138

Appendix 8: Comments Q. 10 - CO_2- Compensation

comments:		44
Negative remark 16 %		
	Ich bezahle schon genug steuern....zwangsabgaben finde ich scheiße. warum soll ich für umweltsünden von china den usa und kanada zahlen?	
	glaube nicht, dass Geldspenden in diesem Bereich was bringen	
	nein, weil das nur ganz einfach das Gewissen Vieler beruhigt ohne ein Umdenken anzustoßen. Naturschutz ok, Müllentsorgung ok, Müllkontollen ok, Geld für CO2 - das ist lächerlich!	
	Nein, Wer garantiert das das geld da auch ankommt, hab noch nie beweise gesehen.	
	ich bin für globale erwärmung. das ganze jahr sommer, echt spitze	
	Is mir einfach egal.	
Hint for implementation (30 %)		
ticket price included	Grundsätzlich ja -> gute Idee!! Allerdings von Veranstalterseiten her steigen die Ticketpreise zum. der "großen" Festivals jährlich um meist ca. €10 - da sollte doch von VA-Seiten was drinnen sein...	
	Diese Abgaben sollten vom Gewinn der Festivalleitung abgehen	
	"Sollte für alle im Preis enthalten sein"	
	Ungerne, wenn der Preis aber in das Festivalticket direkt integriert würde das alles vereinfachen.	
	Ticktes der großen Festivals sind schon so überteuert, es sollte von dem Festbetrag der Tickets etwas für diese Maßnahmen verwendet werden	
	Sollte Pflicht und generell in den Ticketpreis integriert sein.	
	Verpflichtender Beitrag, im Ticketpreis inbegriffen, wäre vielleicht sinnvoller.	
	Gute Idee, aber bei großen Festivals ist der Preis teilweise schon so hoch, dass das von vornherein inbegriffen sein sollte!	
	Der Beitrag sollte sofort in den Ticketpreis einfließen, Eine Preissteigerung von zwei Euro wären jedem egal und das Geld wäre dann fix vorhanden.	
	Sollte verpflichtend sein, wenn jemand 130 euro fuer ein Ticket zahlen kann, kann er auch 5 euro mehr fuer die Umwelt enbehren	
	ob ich das freiwillig machen würde weiß ich nicht. aber wenn die sagen, dass 2-3€ von jedem gekauften ticket an den umweltschutz geht würde ich das gut finden. dann würde mich der zusätzliche preis auch nciht stören. aber freiwillig würde ich das kästchen wohl nicht ankreuzen	
	eine verpflichtende Gebühr einführen für alle Großveranstaltungen (>5000 Personen) von 2€	
	Festivaltickets werden ohnehin immer teurer, davon sollte man einen Teil für Umweltprojekte nutzen und den Besuchern nicht noch mehr Geld abknöpfen	
Info demand (23 %)	Es sollte außerdem erklärt werden, wie genau diese Kompensation aussieht, damit es sich bei einem solchen Beitrag nicht bloß um eine "schwammige" Beruhigung des eigenen Gewissens handelt!	
	"Ist ok, wenn man erfährt für was das Geld verwendet wird"	
	da festivals nicht der hauptverursacher für co2 emissionen sind weiß ich nicht ob das soviel bringt!!!	
	"und transparent dargestellt werden"	
	"würde das Geld 100% in Klimaschutzprojekte fließen? würde genaue Info wünschen, wo das Geld genau hinfließt..."	
	"Nachweis?"	
	"ich will auch sicher sein, dass das Geld dort ankommt und sinnvoll investiert wird"	
	... wenn das geld auch wirklich dort ankommt!! (Kein Ablasshandel um Gewissen zu beruhigen!!)	
	Ja, wenn ich mir sicher sein kann, dass das Geld auch an diese Projekte geht.	
	Ja, wenn das unterstützte Projekt sinnvoll ist	
Indecisive	Geht in Richtung Ablasshandel, über die Wirksamkeit bin ich mir unschlüssig	
Positive remark (11 %)		
	bei differenzierter betrachtung sind die beiden erstgenannten punkte natürlich beide richtig	
	Ja, davon habe ich vorher aber noch nie gehört	
	"2-5 Euro sind nicht so enorm viel Geld. Wenn ich gern auf ein Festival will, dann würde ich mich von 5 Euro mehr nicht abschrecken lassen und das wäre mir die Umwelt doch wert."	
	super idee, ebenfalls wie das müllpfand, dadurch wird mehr an die umwelt gedacht	
	... solange es nicht mehr als 5€ wären!	
Alternative 16 %		

	"Ich würde das Geld lieber in die Forschung am eigenen Festival stecken und schauen wie man dieses im Stromverbrauch etc. so umweltschonend wie möglich zu gestalten."
	"lieber weniger verbrauchen als freikaufen, warum sieht man immernoch so viel klassische lichttechnik anstatt LED?"
	Grundsätzlich finde ich die Idee ganz gut, aber es wäre wohl sinnvoller, mitgebrachte Möbel und all den unnötigen Scheiß der nach einem Festival auf den Zeltplätzen übrig bleibt, zu verbieten. Ebenso sollte Büchsenbier verboten werden, ausschließlich Plastikbecher wie etwa von "CupConcept" erlaubt sein und sowieso dazu angehalten werden, dass der Müll einfacher getrennt wird. Die "Scheißegal-Mentalität" vieler Leute bezüglich Müll sollte besser kontrolliert werden usw. usw.
	5 Euro als Müll - Pfand, überflüssige Konserven sammeln & spenden
	CO_2 Emissionen sind ein super wichtiges Thema. Allerdings bin ich skeptisch ggü. 'Geld für Klimaprojekte'. Das Festival sollte lieber versuchen den eigenen Umweltimpact zu verringern (z.B, Kombitickets Eintritt + Anreise mit der Bahn)
	Lieber vor Ort während des Festivals mehr für den Klimaschutz tun!!
	Einen geringen Geldbetrag zu später ist Nachhaltig keine Lösung! Mein Vorschlag: Sammelbusse organisieren, einen großen gemeinsamen Grillplatz einführe
Lack of information	Wieso entstehen denn durch ein Festival zusätzliche CO_2-Emissionen? Nur wegen Müll? Den würde ich zu Hause doch auch produzieren.
	Nein, weil ich Aufforstungsprojekte nicht als Klimaschutz betrachte. Wenn die Biomasse verrottet wird gebundenes CO_2 wieder frei. Gibt sinnvollere Ansätze

Appendix 9: Comments Q. 8 & Q. 14 - Framework Program

Q 8

Rahmenprogramm — **unnötig:**

"Für mich steht die Musik & die Atmosphäre im Vordergrund. An Mitmachangeboten habe ich kein Interesse."
"Rahmenprogrammpunkte finde ich komplett unwichtig, da man auch so seine Zeit verbringen kann...an den ganzen Kram kann ich privat außerhalb eines Festivals teilnehmen"
"Finde alles unwichtig, da ich wegen der Musik auf ein Festival gehe."
"Festivals sollten sich auf Musik konzentrieren!"; "Schon alles cool, aber doch nicht auf Festivals!"
"Mir geht es bei Musikfestivals primär um die Musik...das Nebenprogramm interessiert mich wenig, egal bei welchem Festival. Einzig das Partyzelt am Abend etwa ist wichtig."
"Auf einem Festival möchte ich Musik hören. Da brauche ich keine Club Med Animation."
"Ich gehe wegen der Musik hin und nicht wegen eines Rahmenprogramms!!"
"Musik und freundliche Leute sind wichtig. Der Rest ist Party"
"Ich gehe auf ein Festival wegen der Musik, habe dann eh "keine Zeit" für was anderes"

Vorschläge:

"Vielseitiges und einfaches Grillen (mehr als nur Bratwurst)"/ Grillkurs oder ein Wettbewerb der Bestern Grillmeister.
"Diskussionsrunden mit Musikern", , "jonglage-workshop", Lesungen, ; "Möglichkeit des Austauschs über gesellschaftspolitisch relevante Themen";
"Theater-Workshop, Streetart-Workshop", "Theaterworkshops"
"DIY aber mehr in Richtung Mode, Accesoires(Nähen,...)"/schmuck herstellen, tshirts bedrucken, schneiden...; "Bau von Schlafplätzen/Hütten aus Pappe, Bau von Möbeln aus Pappe"; Kleinkunst, Malen und Basteln und Kreatives"
" Musik-Workshop"; "Irgendwas mit Musik? !", "Musikmachen"; "Musik machen, zusammen jammen, singen," "Freibier",

Interessiert:

"Kann mir das nicht so recht vorstellen, hört sich aber gut an. Ich glaube, dass müsste ich wenn dann mal spontan ausprobieren, wenn das Angebot an Festivals angeboten wird.";

Q 14

Rather Positive remark	8		24,2 %
	1	interessant, für mich nicht so relevant	
	1	würds mal anschaun	
	1	kommt aufs line-up an, ob ich hingehen würde, aber angebot wäre cool	
	1	Ich würde wahrscheinlich hingehen, wenn auch das Line-Up stimmt.	
	1	Wahrscheinlich würde ich vorbeischauen, wenn es grade keine Band gibt, die mich interessiet.	
	1	Wenn das Lineup passt würde ich auf das Festival gehen und dann auch gerne die Angebote zum Umweltschutz wahrnehmen. Aber nur wegen der Umweltschutzangebote allein würde ich nicht hingehen	
	1	an anderen Themen hätte ich mehr interesse; grundsätzlich ein gutes Angebot	
	1	Menschen auf einem Festival zu Diskussionen um den Klimaschutz zu bringen ist sehr schwer, aber sonst eine gute Idee	
Not fitting to festival	8		24,2%
	1	Mit solchen Themen beschäftige ich mich gerne, aber NICHT auf einem Musikfestival!	
	1	Interesse daran habe ich grundsätzlich, allerdings nicht im Rahmen eines Festivals.	
	1	Ich gehe auf Festivals, um Musik zu hören! Gemüse kann ich Daheim anbauen...	
	1	Fehlplaziert an gestivals find ich. Da will man spaß haben und sich nicht groß gedanken machen	
	1	Auch auf einem Festival ist es von Bedeutung an die Umwelt zu denken jedoch sollte dies durch andere Maßnahmen gedeckt sein und nicht ein aktives Element an einem Festival-Wochenende.	
	1	interessante Punkte, hat meiner Meinung aber nichts auf einem Festival zu suchen. nehme eh sehr wenig vom rahmenprogramm wahr, mir gehts um die Musik, Konzerte und zeit mit Freunden auf dem campingplatz.	
	1	Trotz meines Interesses würde ich eher zu den Konzerten gehen, da ich wegen der Bands auf ein Musikfestival fahre!	
	1	ich finde, dafür ist ein festival der falsche ort	
	1	Warum muss sowas auf nem Festival geschehen? Glaube kaum, dass es ernsthaften Anklang findet	
	1	Ich finde Klima- und Umweltschutz wichtig. Aber ich würde es mir nicht auf dem Festival angucken. Dafür sind die Tickets zu teuer und die Zeit zu kurz, sind ja in meinem Fall , nur 3 Tage im Jahr.	
	1	Die Band sind das Wichtige eines Festivals!	

	1	Interessant, aber auf einem Festival bin ic der Musik wegen
	1	Ich habe kein Interesse mich auf Festivals mit anderen DIngen als Musik, feiern und schlafen zu befassen
	1	Ich finde das nicht den richtigen Rahmen für solche Veranstaltungen. Lieber zu Hause vor Ort
	1	Sehr interessant, für mich auf einem Festival aber nicht der richtige Ort, weil es mir dort mehr auf die Musik und die Zeit mit meinen Freunden ankommt.
	1	Ich finde es interessant und gut, aber auf einem Festival möchte ich einfach eine schöne entspannte Zeit haben und mir dort nicht ständig mit unserer Umwelt konfrontiert werden, das wird man im alltäglichen leben doch schon genug
	1	Bitte bitte nicht auf dem Festival....Es nervt schon genug in der Stadt die grünen Zecken. Ich möchte gern respektiert werden wie ich lebe ich respektiere ja auch die umweltheinis. bitte keinen mit dem erhobenen zeigefinger aktionen auf dem Festival. sucht euch ne andere plattform .-(
	17	0,515151515
Indecisive	7	21 %
	1	Interessant, aber ich würde auf ein 3-Tage-Festival wahrscheinlich nicht hingehen. Bei längeren Aufhalten vielleicht. Grundsätzlich sind Festivals zu kurz um sich vor Ort mit dem Thema zu beschäftigen.
	1	Grundlegend interessant und auch wichtig, nur leider kann ich selbst nicht sagen, ob ich wirklich hingehen würde, wenn ein paar Meter weiter meine Lieblingsbands spielen.
	1	Interessant, habe aber wahrscheinlich eher anderes zu tun.
	1	bei einem guten Line Up finde ich keine Zeit für andere Dinge.
	1	Ich würde zwar hingehen und ich finde es gut,dass sich Festival damit beschäftigen wollen und es weiter geben wollen,jedoch finde ich nicht,dass das unbedingt die Aufgabe eines Festivals ist.
	1	wenn ich zufällig vorbeikomme, ansonsten wohl nich
	1	sehr schwer vorzustellen

Appendix 10: Comments Q. 15 and Q. 16 - Waste

Comments		13
Alternative	Ich nehme nur eigenes Geschirr und eigenes Essen mit. Für Wasser einen auffüllbaren Kanister!	
	Fingerfood??????	
Positive	Sollte es überall geben.	
	Es wär super, wenn man seine Wasserflasche mit reinnehmen dürfte und die immer wieder voll machen könnte.	
	flaschenidee ist gut, beim geschirr käme es aufs material an. normales besteck würde von den meisten sicheheitsdiensten sicher aussortiert	
	eigenes besteck ist eh besser als das plastik zeug	
	Das mit der Flasche finde ich super, sofern es Plastikflaschen sind.[Geschirr finde ich nicht so toll, ebenso wie Glasflaschen, und zwar aus Sicherheitsgründen.]	
doubting	Grundsätzlich eine sehr gute Idee, nur die Umsetzung stelle ich mir für Festivalbesucher etwas nervig vor.	
	flaschenidee ist gut, beim geschirr käme es aufs material an. normales besteck würde von den meisten sicheheitsdiensten sicher aussortiert	
	Logistisch etwas schwierig, auf einem Festival Geschirr mit sich zu tragen.	
	An sich: Super, ich bin dabei. Problem nur: Auf vielen Festivals gibt es vergleichbares ja schon: **Auf dem Southside waren aber viel zu wenig Wasserausgabestellen. Und recht bald prangte ein fetter Zettel dran, auf dem es hieß, das Wasser sei nicht (mehr) zum trinken geeignet.**	
	[Das mit der Flasche finde ich super,]sofern es Plastikflaschen sind. Geschirr finde ich nicht so toll, ebenso wie Glasflaschen, und zwar aus Sicherheitsgründen.	
	Wasser? unnötig!	
	I just wonder who or how washes those dishes and if it doesn't create an even bigger mess.	
	Bringing your own dishes (and forks/knives?) to the festival grounds and carrying them with you all day (even when used/dirty) sounds undesirable. They'd better provide proper dishes and cutlery at food points, which are washed and re-used there.	

Q. 16

Comments			25
Depends on their behaviour		Kommt drauf an ob sich diese Leute als Oberlehrermüllpolizei aufführen oder wirklich freundlich sind und einfach helfen.	
		...sie dürfen nicht zu sehr nerven :D	
		Solange sie nicht zu hart im Tadeln sind. Kann ja auch sein, dass man etwas getrunken hat und sich dadurch mal vertut.	
		an sich ne tolle Sache, wenn die nicht auf die Idee kommen uns zu stressen	
		kommt drauf an, wie sie agieren - mit Witz gut, belehrend nicht	
		Man kann nur hoffen, dass sie Vorbildcharakter haben !	
Own engagement		Ich mache das sowieso schon! Ich bin gegen Einweg-Geschirr etc.	
		ich versuche schon jetzt Müll zu vermeiden	
		ich bin selbst in der Lage, meinen Müll angemessen zu trennen	
		Müll trennen: ja. Teams dafür? nö	
affirmative		Sinnvoll und teilweise auch notwendig. Southside 2011 glich eher einem postapokalyptischen Schlachtfeld als einem Festival (ok, die starken Böen seien mal dahingestellt, aber Türme aus Müll, die von Betrunkenen angebetet werden haben doch etwas... seltsames.) Evtl hätten hier Ordner oder eben solche Teams Abhilfe schaffen können.	
		Gut, beim Festival wird so viel müll produziert, so was würde es einwenig reduzieren. besser als gar nichts.	
		Abgesehen von Umweltaspekten empfinde ich manche Müllberge, vor allem auf dem Campinggelände, als störend. Ein bisschen sanfter Druck von Seiten der Organisation wäre da sicher nicht verkehrt.	
		sie sollten dazu beitragen, dass am ende des festivals jeder seinen müll gerecht entsorgt	
refusing		Oberlehrer zehntausend	

	Ich fände es wohl nervig, ob wohl ich selber auch so meinen Müll richtig entsorge (wenn es denn möglich ist).
	halte ich für schwierig. auf vielen festivals würden sie sicher nur dumm angemacht werden, leider.
	Die Gefahr ist groß, dass Leute denken : "Wozu aufräumen wenns andere für mich machen "
	Zusätzliches Personal, Zusätzliche Anreisen und Emissionen. Diese Personalidee ist Bullshit, weil am Ende des Festivals sowieso alles in einen Container kommt!
	Man könnte sich bevormundet und kontrolliert vorkommen
Alternative	Lieber Müll vermeiden, als Müll trennen
	Wichtig fände ich, dass man nicht 1000 mal Plastikgeschirr holen kann, denn das verschmutzt genau so die welt. Zu beginn des Festivals eine Packung mit 5-10 Gabeln, Messer und Löffel. Wenn man sie verliehrt neue KAUFEN
	Pfandbecher????
Indesicive	Zwiespältig. Auf der einen Seite ist Mülltrennung wichtig, auf der anderen Seite möchte ich mich in dem Moment des "Wegwerfens" auf einem Festival nicht drum kümmern. Sondern es einfach auf den Boden schmeißen (gehört zu meinem Festival-feeling). Am Ende des Festivals würde ich alles aufsammeln und trennen!
	das klingt fast zu deutsch!

Lightning Source UK Ltd.
Milton Keynes UK
UKHW012228300419

341862UK00001B/179/P